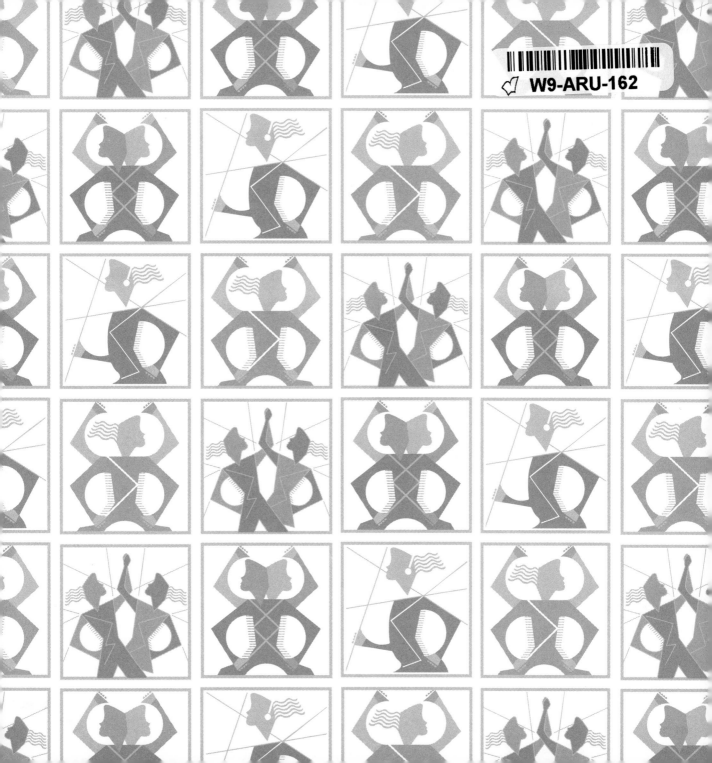

Recipes

for
Success

From Leading Women and Premiere Chefs

This cookbook is a collection of favorite recipes,
which are not necessarily original recipes.

Published by:
Patriots' Trail Girl Scout Council, Inc.

Copyright© 1996
Patriots' Trail Girl Scout Council, Inc.
95 Berkeley Street
Boston, Massachusetts 02116
(617) 482-1078
(800) 882-1662

Library of Congress Catalog Number: 96-92784
ISBN: 0-9654707-0-9

Edited, Designed and Manufactured by:
Favorite Recipes® Press
P.O. Box 305142
Nashville, Tennessee 37230
(800) 358-0560

Manufactured in the United States of America
First Printing: 1996 50,000 copies

The sale of this edition of
Recipes for Success From Leading Women and Premiere Chefs
will benefit girls and young women from all walks of life
as participants in the Girl Scout program.

Thanks

■ ■ ■ ■ ■

Volunteerism is the backbone of Girl Scouting, as well as a key ingredient in the history of the women's movement. As in most volunteer-driven projects, our collaborators are too numerous to mention. We thank each person who helped us make connections with the women in this book; and we thank the contributors for the generosity of their time and willingness to provide words of wisdom.

Special thanks go to Barbara Haber, Curator of Books at Schlesinger Library, Radcliffe College, for her assistance. The Schlesinger Library is the largest collection of the History of Women in America, and has served to document and give voice to the accomplishments of women throughout our society. Barbara's advice and counsel have been very valuable.

The James Beard Foundation provided valuable support, and thanks are also extended to Linda Beaulieu and the College of Culinary Arts of Johnson & Wales University. These two institutions were instrumental in identifying premiere female chefs who have contributed to the book.

Thanks are extended to the Cookbook Committee, volunteers, and staff of Patriots' Trail Girl Scout Council who worked tirelessly to bring this project to a level of excellence under the leadership of Kathy Fleischer.

The multi-dimensional support of the Board of Directors, volunteers, Girl Scouts of the U.S.A., and the more than three million Girl Scouts currently active in the United States, is greatly appreciated.

On behalf of Patriots' Trail, we would like to thank every person who has taken time to mentor a young woman and show her how she could reach her full potential in our society by turning her dreams into reality.

María A. Quiroga
President
Patriots' Trail Girl Scout Council

Laura M. Watkins
Executive Director
Patriots' Trail Girl Scout Council

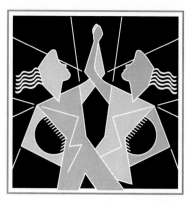

Dedication

■ ■ ■ ■ ■

*R*ecipes for Success From Leading Women and Premiere Chefs *is dedicated to the sixty million women who have found their paths in life with the help of Girl Scouting.*

Since 1912, when Juliette Low founded this movement in the United States, Girl Scouting has been helping girls learn that they can accomplish their goals. The definition of "achievement" has changed dramatically for women. Yet, even in the first Girl Scout handbook, *How Girls Can Help their Country*, employment and career achievement were celebrated through the description of successful women such as Hildegard of Mont Rupert, a "doctoring" woman of the first century, and Miss Mabel Boardman, the head of the Red Cross in the United States during the early 1900s. The handbook notes that "many of the greatest movements for the good of people, and those who have influenced the world the most, have been the work of *one* person." It goes on to say, "One individual often does more than a whole government or an army. One of you girls may someday alter the lives of hundreds of thousands of people."

In 1991, a survey conducted by Louis Harris and Associates found that 64 percent of the women listed in *Who's Who of American Women* had belonged to the Girl Scouts, the factor that proved to be the largest common denominator of these women of distinction. The summary of this study, *Girl Scouts: Its Role In The Lives of American Women of Distinction,* expresses the many ways Girl Scouting shapes individual women, from developing values to increasing self-confidence to having a "real impact on their work or career in later years." With *Recipes for Success,* we celebrate the accomplishments of today's women in very diverse walks of life. This cookbook is meant to salute all of women's contributions to our society, as well as serving as an inspiration to young women just now choosing their personal path in life. May Girl Scouting continue to demonstrate assertive leadership and strong values, as a movement for empowering all young women as they make their mark in our global society!

GIRL SCOUTS®

Foreword

■ ■ ■ ■ ■

*T*hirty years ago and more, a cookbook like this one, made up of recipes by prominent women, would have looked different. More often than not, the contributors would have been the wives of well-known men—politicians, statesmen, athletes, and other public figures. Furthermore, no one would have thought this odd, that women were achieving status only in relationship to how well they married. While it was understood that the behind-the-scenes contributions of women were important, they and their accomplishments tended to be invisible.

All of this has changed. We now want our daughters to reach their full potential as individuals, and we educate and involve them in activities that will deliver this message. We know that society is always the main beneficiary when all of its citizens are trained to be direct contributors toward the greater good. The mission of the Girl Scout movement is to provide young women with inspiration as well as with strategies for achieving their goals. One way of doing this is to assemble a group of prominent women who have made a range of career choices and can lead the way.

The contributors to this book have achieved recognition in many of the fields formerly reserved for men only. Included here are corporate executives, politicians, journalists, and athletes as well as writers, academics, entertainers, and prominent professionals. The group also includes well-known female chefs. Ironically, while most of the routine family cooking has been performed by women, top professional posts almost always have gone to men. It is another sign of our changing times that women are now taking their place within this field as well. The message for young women, of course, is that now that the barriers are down, women finally have the right to choose and then strive for any career they desire.

Barbara Haber

Barbara Haber
Curator of Books
Schlesinger Library, Radcliffe College
Cambridge, Massachusetts

Index of Contributors

■ ■ ■ ■ ■

Table of Contents

■ ■ ■ ■ ■

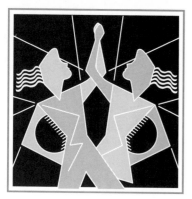

Nutritional Profile Guidelines

■ ■ ■ ■ ■

The editors have attempted to present these family recipes in a form that allows approximate nutritional values to be computed. Persons with dietary or health problems or whose diets require close monitoring should not rely solely on the nutritional information provided. They should consult their physicians or a registered dietitian for specific information.

Abbreviations for Nutritional Profiles

Cal — Calories	T Fat — Total Fat	Sod — Sodium
Prot — Protein	Chol — Cholesterol	g — grams
Carbo — Carbohydrates	Fiber — Dietary Fiber	mg — milligrams

Nutritional information for these recipes is computed from information derived from many sources, including materials supplied by the United States Department of Agriculture, computer databanks, and journals in which the information is assumed to be in the public domain. However, many specialty items, new products and processed foods may not be available from these sources or may vary from the average values used in these profiles. More information on new and/or specific products may be obtained by reading the nutrient labels. Unless otherwise specified, the nutritional profiles of these recipes is based on all measurements being level.

- **Artificial sweeteners** vary in use and strength so should be used "to taste," using the recipe ingredients as a guideline. Sweeteners using aspartame (NutraSweet and Equal) should not be used as a sweetener in recipes involving prolonged heating, which reduces the sweet taste. For further information on the use of these sweeteners, refer to the package.
- **Alcoholic ingredients** have been analyzed for the basic ingredients, although cooking causes the evaporation of alcohol, thus decreasing caloric content.
- **Buttermilk**, **sour cream**, and **yogurt** are the types available commercially.
- **Cake mixes** which are prepared using package directions include 3 eggs and ½ cup oil.
- **Chicken**, cooked for boning and chopping, has been roasted; this method yields the lowest caloric values.
- **Cottage cheese** is cream-style with 4.2% creaming mixture. Dry curd cottage cheese has no creaming mixture.
- **Eggs** are all large. To avoid raw eggs that may carry salmonella as in eggnog or 6-week muffin batter, use an equivalent amount of commerical egg substitute.
- **Flour** is unsifted all-purpose flour.
- **Garnishes**, serving suggestions, and other optional additions and variations are not included in the profiles.
- **Margarine** and **butter** are regular, not whipped or presoftened. Milk is whole milk, 3.5% butterfat. Lowfat milk is 1% butterfat. Evaporated milk is whole milk with 60% of the water removed.
- **Oil** is any type of vegetable cooking oil.
- **Shortening** is hydrogenated vegetable shortening.
- **Salt** and other ingredients to taste as noted in the ingredients have not been included in the nutritional profiles.
- If a choice of ingredients has been given, the nutritional profiles reflect the first option. If a choice of amounts has been given, the nutritional profiles reflect the greater amount.

Leading The Way

Women carry the spirit of our foremothers; we run
an extended marathon; we balance multiple roles
in society. We measure our success by the doors we open
for our daughters, so they may know ever rising achievement.

Anne Finucane

A senior vice president and director of corporate marketing and commun-ications for Boston-based Fleet Financial Group, Anne Finucane oversees Fleet's corporate marketing, advertising, research, charitable giving, community and media relations, and the corporate economics unit. She is a veteran communications executive with more than two decades of experience as a marketing and communications professional. Anne Finucane has been active in several community organizations, and has served on the Conservation Law Foundation and the board of the International Center for Journalists.

■

Live life fully. Believe in yourself and your ability to do what is needed. Let your internal compass be your guide.

Baked Brie

■ ■ ■ ■ ■

This recipe may be adapted to fit the size and tastes of the group.

1 (4-inch) wheel brie
$\frac{1}{3}$ cup (or more) packed brown sugar
$\frac{1}{3}$ cup apricot preserves
$\frac{1}{4}$ cup raisins (optional)
$\frac{1}{3}$ cup sliced almonds or chopped pecans or walnuts

*S*lice the white rind from the top of the brie, leaving the rind on bottom and sides intact. Place the brie in a baking pan. Combine the brown sugar, preserves, raisins and almonds in a small bowl and mix well. Spread the mixture over the brie. Bake at 350 degrees for 10 to 15 minutes or until the brie is soft and the brown sugar is melted. Serve with crackers, French bread toasts, sliced pears and fresh strawberries. Use a spoon and knife for serving ease.

Serves 4

Sweet Potato Dip

■ ■ ■ ■ ■

2 cups fat-free sour cream
$\frac{1}{2}$ cup packed brown sugar
Cinnamon to taste
Nutmeg to taste
3 sweet potatoes

Combine the sour cream, brown sugar, cinnamon and nutmeg in a bowl and mix well. Spoon into a serving bowl and place on a platter. Cut the sweet potatoes into pieces the size of matchsticks. Arrange on the platter.

Serves 16

Suzanne P. Vieira

A noted lecturer on the topic of nutrition and disease prevention, Suzanne Vieira is a registered dietitian and Chairperson of the Foodservice Academic Studies Department at Johnson & Wales University's College of Culinary Arts in Providence, Rhode Island. She is a member of the American Culinary Federation, the American School Foodservice Association, the American Dietetic Association, and a host of other professional organizations. Recently Suzanne was selected to teach school food service personnel from around the country how to prepare school lunches that are essentially lower in fat, sodium, and cholesterol and higher in vegetables, fruits, and grains. Before going to Johnson & Wales, she worked as an outpatient hospital dietitian and as a cardiac rehabilitation nutritionist. She has lectured at Harvard Medical School and at the USDA Human Nutrition Research Center at Tufts University.

Alice Waters

Chef and owner of Chez Panisse for over twenty-five years, Alice Waters has kept her philosophy of serving the highest-quality products according to the season. With a network of farmers and ranchers, Chez Panisse is assured a steady supply of pure and fresh ingredients. This allows Alice Waters to keep serving a five-course, fixed-price menu that changes daily and remains at the heart of her philosophy. Featuring an open kitchen, a wood-burning pizza oven, and an à la carte menu, the upstairs cafe was opened by her in 1980. In 1984, Cafe Fanny, a stand-up cafe serving breakfast and lunch, opened a few miles from the restaurant. Alice Waters is the author of six Chez Panisse cookbooks, serves on several boards and organizations, and is the recipient of numerous awards. She received the 1992 James Beard Foundation Awards for Best Chef in America and Best Restaurant in America.

Tomato Salsa

■ ■ ■ ■ ■

I like to make a lot of salsa for guacamole, quesadillas, and enough for my dad to eat with chips.

6 ripe tomatoes
1/2 small onion
3 tablespoons finely chopped cilantro leaves
1 large or 2 small cloves of garlic, finely chopped
1/2 teaspoon salt
Juice of 1/2 lime

*R*inse and core the tomatoes. Slice the tomatoes and coarsely chop. Slice the onion and coarsely chop. Combine the tomatoes, onion, cilantro, garlic, salt and lime juice in a bowl and mix well. Taste and adjust the seasonings. Let stand at room temperature for 15 minutes to enhance the flavor. May add chopped chiles for a spicier flavor.

Makes 2 1/2 cups

Alice Waters, *Fanny at Chez Panisse*, HarperCollins, 1992, New York, New York.

Shari Lewis' Mozzarella Marinara

■ ■ ■ ■ ■

16 ounces mozzarella cheese, cut into ¹/₂-inch slices
2 eggs, lightly beaten
¹/₂ cup flour
1 cup herb-seasoned bread crumbs
Olive oil for frying
1 (10-ounce) can pizza sauce, heated
1 (2-ounce) can flat anchovies

Dip the cheese slices in the eggs and roll in the flour; coat both sides with the bread crumbs. Arrange on a tray. Freeze for 20 minutes. Pour olive oil into a skillet to a depth of ¹/₄ inch. Preheat the oil. Fry the cheese slices in the hot oil until brown and crisp on both sides, turning occasionally. Drain on paper towels. Arrange on a serving platter. Top each cheese slice with the warm pizza sauce and an anchovy strip.

Serves 8

■

My folks reduced most of their lessons for me to short, sweet statements that are easy to understand and hard to forget. I live by them to this day. They include: *If you can't take it, you can't make it. *You are what you eat (really)! *The day begins the night before. (I lay out my clothes the night before and make sure I get at least eight hours of sleep.) *God helps those who help themselves. *Wouldn't the woods be silent if only the best birds sang? (This has always encouraged me to participate at my own level, whatever that level may be.) I hear these phrases in my ear, as I live all the stages of my life. Clearly, the eternal verity that I learned while studying Spanish in high school is not a cliché, but the truth: "Lo que bien se apriende, no se olvida," which means: that which is well learned is never forgotten!

Shari Lewis

An accomplished actress, producer, orchestra conductor, recording artist, ventriloquist, puppeteer, and author, Shari Lewis is best known for entertaining millions of children and their families with Lamb Chop for over thirty years. Helping to set the standard for family-oriented entertainment, she is the recipient of several awards, including eleven Emmys and the prestigious Action for Children's Television Award. Shari Lewis served on the National Board of the Girl Scouts of the U.S.A., which honored her with the Grace Award. A fourth season of her award-winning series, "Lamb Chop's Play-Along," is currently in production and airs nationally on PBS.

Peter Simon

Rosabeth Moss Kanter

Professor of Business Administration at the Harvard University School of Business Administration, Rosabeth Moss Kanter has published twelve books and over 150 articles, including award-winners like When Giants Learn to Dance: Mastering the Challenges of Strategy Management and Careers in the 1990's *and* Men and Women of the Corporation. *She has taught at Harvard, Yale, and Brandeis; co-founded Goodmeasure, Inc., a consulting firm; and has received numerous awards and honorary degrees, including several Woman of the Year awards. She is also the renowned author of* A Tale of "O": On Being Different, *and has served on numerous government commissions and public interest organizations.*

Snake Bites

■ ■ ■ ■ ■

Rosabeth Moss Kanter enjoys ordering take-out food from her favorite restaurant, The Cottonwood Cafe, Cambridge, Massachusetts. This recipe was provided by Richard Sierra, head chef.

12 large pickled jalapeños
¼ cup shredded Monterey Jack cheese
12 large shrimp (16 to 20 count), peeled, deveined, grilled
1 cup (about) flour   5 eggs, lightly beaten
3 cups yellow cornmeal
1 quart corn or vegetable oil for deep-frying

*S*lit the jalapeños and remove the seeds. Stuff the jalapeños with the cheese. Place 1 grilled shrimp in each jalapeño; secure with a wooden pick. Roll in flour, dip in eggs and coat with the cornmeal. Heat the oil in a skillet to 375 degrees. Deep-fry the stuffed jalapeños until golden brown; drain.

Serves 6

■

One of my favorite lessons of life is that "everything can look like a failure in the middle." Success is hard work; don't give up "in the middle." Persist, persevere, get help, try again—and more often than not, you can convert a possible failure into resounding success. And, "share the wealth." We don't succeed alone. Leaders need to know how to involve others, support others, and get sponsored by them, and then share the credit and the recognition. Make friends, find allies, and see that everyone can get more done by collaborating than by operating alone.

Mom's Basic BBQ Sauce

■ ■ ■ ■ ■

I have friends who make multiple batches of Mom's Basic BBQ Sauce and keep it in the fridge all year round—when they're not giving it away to friends. The sauce has a hearty, full flavor that complements just about anything—try dipping a slice of toasted garlic bread into it. Use as a basting sauce for vegetable kabobs as well as steaks, pork chops, chicken, ribs, hot dogs, hamburgers, and shrimp.

1 cup strong coffee   ¹/₂ cup packed brown sugar
¹/₂ cup Worcestershire sauce
¹/₃ cup cider vinegar
1¹/₂ cups catsup   ¹/₂ cup corn oil

*C*ombine the coffee, brown sugar, Worcestershire sauce and vinegar in a saucepan and mix well. Whisk in the catsup. Bring to a boil; reduce heat. Simmer for 5 minutes, stirring frequently. Whisk in the corn oil. Let stand until cool. Store, covered, in the refrigerator for up to 2 months.

Makes 4 cups

■

I was extremely lucky to have parents who gave me the inner strength to believe in myself; to expect to accomplish whatever I wanted to do. On a day-to-day level, I tape quotes I clip from magazines and newspapers to my computer and my bookcase to inspire me when I need spurring on. Two of my favorites: the first, from a business woman in a leadership position, "Deal compassionately with everyone who looks to you for commitment and nourishment"; and the second, from an extraordinarily successful car salesman, "I reject rejection. A 'No' is not a 'No' to me. It's simply an opportunity to get a 'Yes.'" So take these opportunities and make them your own.

Leslie Beal Bloom

Past President of the International Association of Culinary Professionals, Leslie Beal Bloom is a food writer, recipe consultant, and cooking instructor. In these endeavors, she shares her love of cooking with her culinary expertise. Leslie is a contributing editor for Simply Seafood *magazine, and her food articles have appeared in the* Washington Post, *the* New York Times, Food and Wine, Gourmet, *and many other national publications. In her spare time, she kayaks the Arctic in search of exotic seafood.*

Elaine Cwynar

A true Renaissance woman, Elaine Cwynar knows how to navigate herself around the kitchen. A culinary arts teacher at Johnson & Wales University in Providence, Rhode Island, she has served as chef steward aboard the Regis Maris, a 145-foot barque sailing vessel, sailing through the Panama Canal to the Galapagos Islands on a five-month trip, and aboard the Westward, a 125-foot sailing research vessel, to the Northern Canadian Provinces for ten weeks. Continuing to combine her love for cooking and her passion for sailing, Elaine Cwynar was the cook/navigator on board a cruising racer in the Newport-to-Bermuda Race in June, 1996. When she is not sailing or traveling around the world, she likes to cook food from her homeland, Poland.

Beet Soup
(Barszcz)

■ ■ ■ ■ ■

8 red beets, peeled, thinly sliced
1 onion, sliced
1 rib celery, sliced
1 large carrot, chopped
1½ to 2 quarts beef stock
1 teaspoon apple cider vinegar
1 teaspoon sugar
Salt and pepper to taste
2 cups sour cream
8 ounces Polish sausage, coarsely crumbled, cooked, drained
2 hard-cooked eggs, chopped
3 slices rye bread, torn

*C*ombine the beets, onion, celery and carrot in a stockpot. Add just enough stock to cover. Stir in the vinegar. Cook over medium heat for 1 hour or until the beets are tender, stirring occasionally. Add the sugar, salt and pepper and mix well. Strain, discarding the vegetables. Combine the sour cream and ½ cup of the hot liquid in a bowl and mix well. Add to the hot liquid in the stockpot and mix well. Cover to keep warm. Combine the sausage, eggs and bread in a bowl and mix well. Ladle the hot soup mixture into soup bowls. Top with the sausage mixture. May add additional vinegar to each bowl.

Serves 8

Broccoli and Cauliflower Soup

■ ■ ■ ■ ■

1 large onion, chopped
2 or 3 shallots, chopped
1 or 2 ribs celery
1 clove of garlic, minced
¹/₄ cup margarine
¹/₄ cup flour
8 cups chicken broth
1 bunch broccoli, peeled, chopped
Flowerets of 1 head cauliflower

*S*auté the onion, shallots, celery and garlic in the margarine in a stockpot until brown. Stir in the flour. Cook for 3 to 5 minutes, stirring constantly. Add the broth gradually and mix well. Stir in the broccoli and cauliflower. Cook for 30 to 40 minutes or until the broccoli and cauliflower are tender, stirring occasionally. Remove ¹/₄ of the broccoli and cauliflower with a slotted spoon to a bowl and set aside. Process the remaining mixture in a blender until puréed. Return to the stockpot. Add the reserved broccoli and cauliflower. Cook just until heated through, stirring frequently. Ladle into soup bowls. Serve with sour cream and/or shredded cheese.

Serves 8

Patty Stonesifer

As senior vice-president leading Microsoft's Interactive Media Division, Patty Stonesifer is responsible for the creation and marketing of interactive entertainment and information products across a variety of media, including the Internet. Formed in February 1996, the Interactive Media Division offers a wide range of software and on-line products in the broad categories of kids, entertainment, information, and reference. Some award-winning titles in Stonesifer's division include Microsoft 3D Movie Maker, Microsoft Flight Simulator, and the Microsoft Encarta Encyclopedia.

■

Now is a very exciting time for women in technology. We have a unique opportunity to shape the future of the industry, and to work in a field that combines not only technology, but art, education, music, history, and communications.

Brooke Medicine Eagle

An enrolled member of the Crow Indian tribe in Montana, Brooke Medicine Eagle is primarily identified as a global family Earthkeeper, dedicated to nurturing and renewing the Circle of Life through the growth and healing of our two-legged family on Mother Earth. At home in the beautiful Flathead Valley, Brooke is the creator of EagleSong, a series of spiritually-oriented wilderness camps. She is also the founder of both the FlowerSong Project, which promotes a sustainable, ecologically-sound path upon Mother Earth for seven generations of children, and the Rainbow Peoples Project, a cross-cultural educational development foundation.

Curried Ginger Carrot Soup

■ ■ ■ ■ ■

3 large carrots, coarsely chopped
^{1}/$_2$ cup coarsely chopped onion
1 tablespoon minced gingerroot
2 tablespoons butter
2 teaspoons salt
1 teaspoon curry
^{1}/$_4$ teaspoon pepper
4 cups water
2 tablespoons sherry
1 tablespoon honey
Juice of ^{1}/$_2$ lemon

*S*auté the carrots, onion and gingerroot in the butter in a saucepan for 3 to 4 minutes or until the onion is tender. Add the salt, curry and pepper. Sauté briefly. Stir in the water, sherry and honey. Simmer, covered, for 45 minutes or until the carrots are tender, stirring occasionally. Process the carrot mixture in a blender until puréed. Return the mixture to the saucepan. Stir in the lemon juice. Ladle into soup bowls. May substitute parsnips, rutabaga or squash for the carrots.

Serves 6

■

Remember that the Earth is your true mother, and remember to love and honor Her as you continue to learn Her special and profound lessons. You are related to all Earth's children—everything on this beautiful planet—so remember to love, honor, and care for all these relations as well.

Johnny Bob's Chili

■ ■ ■ ■ ■

1 to 1¹/₂ pounds ground beef
1 potato, chopped
¹/₂ green bell pepper, chopped
¹/₂ cup chopped onion   Chili powder to taste
Sliced mushrooms to taste
2 or 3 (16-ounce) cans chili beans
¹/₂ (14-ounce) bottle catsup
2 (8-ounce) cans tomato sauce
1 (6-ounce) can tomato paste
Pepper and red wine to taste
1 to 2 tablespoons (about) jalapeño relish, or to taste

*B*rown the ground beef with the next 5 ingredients in a saucepan, stirring until the ground beef is crumbly; drain. Stir in the chili beans, catsup, tomato sauce, tomato paste, pepper and red wine. Add the jalapeño relish 1 tablespoon at a time until of the desired degree of spiciness. Simmer, covered, until the potatoes are tender, stirring occasionally. Ladle into chili bowls. Serve with a green salad or fresh fruit and crackers.

Serves 8

■

I'd like to pass along some advice I once heard from another professional business woman that really works for me: When you get up in the morning you have to imagine everything you have to do, all of your responsibilities, each as little balls. You throw them all up in the air each day, and the ones you catch are the ones you deal with that day. The rest you leave on the floor—you can deal with those tomorrow because they'll still be there, and tomorrow's another day.

Cheryl Womack

In the basement of her home in 1983, Cheryl Womack founded VCW, Inc., an insurance agency designed to meet the insurance needs of a specific trucking industry segment. Soon after, she founded a third party claims administrator (Preferred Administrative Services, Inc.) to process claims for VCW, Inc. Both companies were established to serve the over 8,000 members of the National Association of Independent Truckers (NAIT). Today, Cheryl Womack's companies report gross revenues in excess of $46 million and employ more than 80 people. Womack, who is involved in many professional and civic organizations, says that being one of eleven children has helped give her what it takes to be an entrepreneur.

Senator Kay Bailey Hutchison

The first woman to represent the state of Texas in the U.S. Senate, Senator Kay Bailey Hutchison was elected in June of 1993 by the widest margin ever cast against a sitting, incumbent Senator. In November, 1994, she was re-elected to a full, six-year term. In 1976, President Gerald Ford appointed her Vice Chairman of the National Transportation Safety Board. In 1990, Senator Hutchison was elected Texas State Treasurer, and, in 1995, she was named a deputy Majority Whip and co-chair of the Senate GOP Regulatory Reform Task Force. Serving on the Armed Services Committee, she became the first woman to serve on the Senate Select Committee on Intelligence.

■

America is the greatest nation on Earth to be a woman. Each of you has the potential to be a leader. Hard work and determination to succeed will take you far in life and will open the door to unlimited opportunities.

Kay's Shadywood Showdown Chili

■ ■ ■ ■ ■

2 tablespoons olive oil
2 medium yellow onions, chopped
2 green peppers, chopped
Salt and freshly ground pepper to taste
Garlic powder to taste
2¹/₂ pounds ground sirloin
4 tablespoons mole sauce
2 (8-ounce) cans tomato sauce
2 cups water
3 tablespoons chili powder mix
1 (16-ounce) can kidney beans, drained
1 tablespoon chili powder mix, or to taste

*H*eat 1 tablespoon of the olive oil in a skillet over medium heat until hot. Sauté ¹/₂ of the onions and ¹/₂ of the green peppers in the hot oil until the onions are tender. Stir in the salt, pepper and garlic powder. Brown the ground sirloin in a skillet, stirring until crumbly; drain. Add the onion mixture and 3 tablespoons of the mole sauce and mix well. Spoon into a stockpot. Add the tomato sauce, water and 3 tablespoons chili powder mix and mix well. Bring to a boil; reduce heat. Stir in remaining 1 tablespoon mole sauce. Simmer for 1 hour, stirring occasionally. Adjust seasonings. Sauté remaining onions and green peppers in remaining 1 tablespoon olive oil in a skillet for 2 minutes. Stir into the ground sirloin mixture. Add the beans and 1 tablespoon chili powder mix and mix well. Cook for 15 minutes longer, stirring occasionally. Ladle into chili bowls. Garnish with shredded Cheddar cheese, chopped green onions and/or minced jalapeños. May purchase mole sauce in the Mexican food section of most grocery stores.

Serves 8

Pamela Peters' Chili

■ ■ ■ ■ ■

1¹/₂ pounds lean ground beef
2 ounces jalapeños, cut into ¹/₄-inch pieces
6 ounces red bell peppers, cut into ¹/₄-inch pieces
6 ounces yellow bell peppers, cut into ¹/₄-inch pieces
8 ounces onions, cut into ¹/₄-inch pieces
2 tablespoons olive oil   4 cloves of garlic, minced
2 tablespoons chili powder
1 tablespoon cumin
1¹/₂ teaspoons oregano
1 teaspoon each freshly ground black pepper and salt
¹/₂ teaspoon crushed red pepper
2 pounds fresh tomatoes, peeled, seeded, chopped
1 (15-ounce) can tomato purée
8 ounces black beans, cooked
¹/₄ bunch cilantro, chopped
2 cups sour cream   Juice of 1 lime
8 ounces Monterey Jack cheese, shredded
6 sprigs of cilantro

Pamela Peters

A certified executive chef and certified culinary educator, Pamela Peters is also an expert on spices. A member of the McCormick Spice Company Advisory Council, she is frequently called upon to test new blends of spices, from Thai to Tex-Mex. This expertise has evolved from her position as sous chef at the Hyatt Hotel in Atlanta, where she made twenty-five gallons of chili—enough for five hundred people—at a time.

*B*rown the ground beef in a stockpot over medium heat, stirring until crumbly; drain. Sauté the jalapeños, bell peppers and onions in olive oil in a skillet until tender. Stir in the garlic. Sauté for 1 minute. Add the seasonings. Cook for several minutes, stirring frequently. Stir into the ground beef. Add the tomatoes and tomato purée and mix well. Cook for 30 to 45 minutes or to the desired consistency, stirring occasionally. Stir in beans and ¹/₄ bunch chopped cilantro. Simmer for 15 minutes, stirring occasionally. Ladle into chili bowls. Top with a mixture of sour cream and lime juice, cheese and cilantro sprig.

Serves 6

Jewell Jackson McCabe

Chairman and founder of the National Coalition of 100 Black Women, Jewell Jackson McCabe has wide-ranging experience in both the private and public sectors. She has served as director on a variety of boards, as a Presidential and gubernatorial appointee, and as a consultant to major corporations She was appointed by President Clinton to the U.S. Holocaust Memorial Council, where she served as a member of the Education and Community Outreach Committees. Governor Mario M. Cuomo appointed Ms. McCabe to the New York State Council on Fiscal and Economic Priorities.

■

Through art, education or hobbies (reading, sports, crafts, etc.), develop projects with a distinct beginning and end. Introduce discipline, patience and organization to your lives, so they become habitual rituals you apply to every aspect of your life. Be aware. Learn the consequences of your actions.

Spicy Crab Soup

■ ■ ■ ■ ■

2 pounds new potatoes
1 bunch fresh spinach
1 tablespoon virgin olive oil
6 cloves of garlic, crushed
3 shallots, thinly sliced
6 (14-ounce) cans chicken broth
1 cup dry white wine
2 tablespoons Creole seasoning, or to taste
2 teaspoons ground cumin
1 teaspoon curry powder
Salt to taste
1 pound Maryland blue lump crab meat, drained, flaked
1 bunch scallions, chopped

*C*ombine the new potatoes with enough water to cover in a saucepan. Cook until tender; drain. Chill, covered, in a bowl in the refrigerator. Rinse the spinach and tear each leaf into thirds. Heat a skillet over low heat for 2 to 3 minutes. Add the olive oil. Sauté the garlic and shallots in the hot olive oil until tender and light brown. Remove from heat. Combine broth, white wine, Creole seasoning, cumin and curry powder in a saucepan. Bring to a boil; reduce heat. Simmer for 10 to 15 minutes, stirring occasionally. Peel and chop the potatoes. Add the potatoes and garlic mixture to the broth mixture and mix well. Season with salt. Add the spinach and crab meat just before serving. Ladle into soup bowls. Sprinkle with scallions. May substitute any shellfish, fish or cooked fowl for the crab meat.

Serves 8

Cold Gazpacho
■ ■ ■ ■ ■

*This is a delightful, cold, fresh vegetable soup
for a warm summer day.*

**6 to 7 fresh tomatoes, finely chopped
2 onions, finely chopped
2 medium green bell peppers, finely chopped
2 medium cucumbers, peeled, seeded, finely chopped
2 to 3 cloves of garlic, finely chopped
1 small bunch cilantro, finely chopped
1 small bunch basil, finely chopped
1 (46-ounce) can vegetable juice cocktail
Juice of 2 lemons   3 to 4 tablespoons virgin olive oil
Lemon pepper to taste   1 avocado, chopped
Sour cream to taste**

*C*ombine the tomatoes, onions, green peppers, cucumbers, garlic, cilantro and basil in a bowl and mix gently. Stir in the vegetable juice cocktail, lemon juice, olive oil and lemon pepper. Chill, covered, in the refrigerator. Ladle the gazpacho over the avocado in soup bowls. Top with sour cream. May add additional vegetable juice cocktail for a thinner consistency. May substitute salt and pepper for the lemon pepper.

Serves 10

■

*Be yourself. Find a role model and mentor with whom you can
share and discuss your ideas about life and your goals. Live by the
values learned in your family and in Girl Scouting.*

Elinor J. Ferdon

Elected to Girl Scouts of the U.S.A.'s National Board of Directors in 1978, Elinor J. Ferdon most recently was First Vice President, chair of the Executive Committee of GSUSA. She assumed the presidency of the World Foundation of Girl Guides and Girl Scouts, Inc., in 1991. She also chaired the 1996 World Conference of the World Association of Girl Guides and Girl Scouts (WAGGGS). Elinor currently serves on the boards of Summit Bancorp and Summit Bank, the United Way of America Board of Governors and the Liberty Science Center as vice chair. She is Trustee Emeritus of Farleigh Dickinson University and immediate past member of the executive committee of the National Urban League. Her distinguished efforts in community leadership have prompted numerous awards, including the Alexis de Tocqueville Award from the United Way of America and the Woman of Achievement Award from Douglass College.

Bachrach

Linda S. Wilson

On July 1, 1989, Linda Wilson
became the seventh president of
Radcliffe College. She has a Ph.D. in
inorganic chemistry from the
University of Wisconsin and is the
recipient of numerous awards and
Honorary Doctorate degrees. She now
leads an educational institution
dedicated to the advancement of
women in society through education,
research, and public policy.

■

*Success and service depend on
recognizing, choosing, and using
opportunities thoughtfully and creatively.
Be alert for opportunities, both small and
large. Learn to recognize them and to
choose among them. Think about what
they offer to you personally as well as
what possibilities they offer you to be of
service to others. Take note of what you
learn in pursuing opportunities and fold
that into your assessment and choice of
other opportunities that come along.*

Creole Gumbo New Orleans Style

■ ■ ■ ■ ■

*This easy recipe, handed down over generations, was given to
me by my mother-in-law the year I married her son. I consider it
a family treasure. The seasonings can be adjusted to be mild or
spicy. The gumbo may be served as a first course or entrée.
Double or triple the recipe since it freezes well, and most people
ask for seconds. All the measurements are approximate.*

1 onion, finely chopped
4 ounces ham, chopped
3 tablespoons bacon drippings or shortening
12 ounces fresh okra, finely sliced
Lemon juice to taste
1 (16-ounce) can tomato sauce
8 ounces (or more) shrimp, peeled, deveined
3 or 4 fresh crabs
1 teaspoon filé powder
1 bay leaf
Salt and hot pepper sauce to taste

*S*auté onion and ham in bacon drippings in a stockpot
until the onion is light brown. Add the okra and lemon
juice (lemon juice keeps the okra from becoming slimy). Fry the
okra until all sliminess disappears (this is the secret of good
gumbo). Stir in the tomato sauce. Cook just until the mixture
begins to bubble, stirring frequently. Add enough hot water to
make of the desired consistency and mix well. Bring to a boil.
Cook for 15 minutes, stirring occasionally. Add the remaining
ingredients. Cook for 30 minutes or until of the desired
consistency, stirring occasionally. Discard the bay leaf. Serve
over hot rice in bowls with French bread and salad.

Serves 4

Minestrone

■ ■ ■ ■ ■

1 cup chopped onion
1 cup chopped carrot
¹⁄₄ to ¹⁄₂ cup olive oil
1 cup chopped celery
2 cups chopped potatoes
2 cups sliced zucchini
2 cups chopped red or green cabbage
1 to 2 (14-ounce) cans chicken stock
1 (16-ounce) can whole tomatoes
1 (16-ounce) can chopped tomatoes
6 (8-ounce) cans tomato sauce
6 cups (about) water
1 cup cooked green beans
1 cup cooked white cannelloni beans
Grated Parmesan cheese to taste

Sauté the onion and carrot in the olive oil in a stockpot until of the desired degree of doneness. Add the celery, potatoes and zucchini and mix well. Sauté until of the desired degree of doneness. Add the cabbage, stock, tomatoes and tomato sauce and enough water to make of the desired consistency and mix well. Simmer until of the desired consistency, stirring occasionally. Add the green beans and cannelloni beans just before serving. Cook until heated through. Ladle into soup bowls. Sprinkle with grated Parmesan cheese. May substitute broth or a combination of broth and water for the water and spaghetti sauce for the tomato sauce.

Serves 10

Joan Benoit Samuelson

An athlete, coach, motivational speaker, clinician, author, and mother of two, Joan Benoit Samuelson received the Olympic Gold Medal in 1984, the year of the first women's Olympic marathon. She won the Boston Marathon in 1979, setting a new world record, and broke her own world record in the 1983 Boston Marathon. Joan has conducted numerous running, health and fitness clinics throughout the United States and the world.

■

Live your dreams/Believe in yourself.

Dominique Vobillon

Deborah Madison

The founding chef of San Francisco's Greens Restaurant, Deborah Madison is the author of two award-winning books, The Greens Cookbook *and* The Savory Way *(which was voted* Cookbook of the Year *by the IACP).* She is also the author of the soon-to-be-released books, The Vegetarian Table: America *and* Deborah Madison's Essential Vegetarian Cookbook. *A contributor to several food magazines, Deborah also teaches cooking throughout the United States and helps run the Santa Fe Farmer's Market.*

■

My advice in cooking applies to life as well—don't be afraid to experiment and trust your own senses! Who else but you can say whether your soup has enough salt, or your life enough spice? Truly relying on yourself while keeping your mind open to life's possibilities is a balancing act—and hopefully a recipe for success!

Basic Potato Soup

■ ■ ■ ■ ■

This is a great first soup for a novice cook, or a fast and easy one for the more experienced. It costs practically nothing with ordinary boiling potatoes—a little more with fancy potatoes, such as Yellow Finns.

2 tablespoons olive oil, butter or a mixture
2 onions, finely chopped   3 small bay leaves
2 pounds potatoes, peeled
1½ teaspoons salt   9 cups water
Salt and freshly ground pepper to taste
2 tablespoons chopped fresh parsley
Grated Parmesan cheese to taste

*H*eat the olive oil in a heavy stockpot over medium heat. Add the onions and bay leaves. Sauté over low heat. Quarter potatoes lengthwise, then slice thinly. Add to stockpot. Sauté over high heat for 10 minutes or until the onions begin to brown and a glaze forms on the bottom of the stockpot. Stir in 1½ teaspoons salt and 1 cup water. Deglaze stockpot. Add the remaining 8 cups water. Bring to a boil; reduce heat. Simmer, loosely covered, for 30 minutes or until the potatoes are tender, stirring occasionally. Season with salt and pepper. Stir in the parsley. Discard the bay leaves. Ladle into soup bowls. Sprinkle with Parmesan cheese. For a thicker consistency, press 1 or 2 cups of the soup through a food mill and return to the stockpot. There are all kinds of ingredients that taste good in this soup. Some favorites are 1 or 2 heads of roasted garlic, cooked along with the potatoes; sautéed mustard greens or spinach, added at the end of cooking; 2 cups chopped parsley; a few spoonfuls of cream; or replace a portion of the potatoes with any good root vegetable.

Serves 6

Winter Squash and Pear Soup

■ ■ ■ ■ ■

Heidi Insalata Krahling

¼ cup unsalted butter   3 leek bulbs, chopped
1 small yellow onion, chopped
1 turban squash, peeled, cut into ½-inch pieces
8 cups chicken stock   1 cinnamon stick
3 comice pears, peeled, cut into ½-inch pieces
1 tablespoon salt   Zest of 2 oranges
1 (1-inch) piece gingerroot, peeled, grated
½ teaspoon allspice   Juice of 1 lemon
Salt and pepper to taste
1 cup (about) crème fraîche or sour cream
Freshly grated nutmeg to taste

*M*elt the butter in a 10-quart stockpot. Add the leeks and onion. Sauté until tender. Add the squash, stock and cinnamon stick. Bring to a boil; reduce heat. Simmer until the squash is tender, stirring occasionally. Add the pears, 1 tablespoon salt, orange zest, gingerroot and allspice and mix well. Simmer for 5 minutes, stirring occasionally. Discard the cinnamon stick. Purée the mixture in a blender. Return to stockpot. Season with lemon juice, salt and pepper to taste. Heat just until warm. Ladle into soup bowls. Top each serving with a mixture of crème fraîche and nutmeg.

Serves 14

■

Currently the Executive Chef at the Smith Ranch Homes in San Rafael, California, Heidi Insalata Krahling has owned and operated several restaurants since 1978. She has instructed cooking at the Tante Marie's Cooking School in San Francisco, has been recognized as a "Rising Star" by San Francisco Focus, *and celebrated as one of* USA Today's *"Best Women Chefs of 1988." Heidi Krahling is also involved in several community organizations, having served as Restaurant Coordinator for the American Heart Association, the Marin Agency for Retarded Citizens (MARC) and SOS Taste of the Nation, one of San Francisco's largest charity events.*

I, for one, am primarily interested in the effect that my creations have on those who might enjoy them. For me, food is a means of expression and a way of giving comfort and joy to others. My experience is that a great many women share this philosophy and it is this nurturing aspect of food that has led many of us into this profession.

Monique A. Barbeau

A native of Vancouver, British Columbia, Monique Barbeau is the chef of Fullers in the Sheraton Seattle Hotel and Towers. Since she has taken charge of the kitchen, Fullers has been rated as one of the top restaurants in the country by Conde Nast Traveler. *In 1995, the readers of* Seattle *magazine voted her Seattle's Best Chef. A graduate of the Culinary Institute of America, Monique Barbeau previously worked at three New York City four-star restaurants, and, in 1994, the James Beard Foundation named her Perrier-Jouët Best Chef of the Pacific Northwest. She received the 1995 Unsung Hero Award from the March of Dimes for her contributions to the annual Gourmet Gala fundraiser.*

Watercress Soup
■ ■ ■ ■ ■

2 cups chopped white onions
¹/₂ cup butter
6 cups chicken stock
2 potatoes, peeled, cut into 8 pieces
1 pound finnan haddie   1¹/₂ cups whipping cream
3 bunches watercress, stems removed
2 tablespoons lemon juice   Salt and pepper to taste

*S*auté the onions in butter in a saucepan over medium heat until tender. Add the stock and potatoes. Bring to a boil; reduce heat. Simmer for 20 minutes or until the potatoes are tender. Steep the fish in the whipping cream in a saucepan until warm. Remove from heat. Let stand for 20 minutes to allow flavors to marry. Strain, reserving the cream. Reserve the fish for another purpose. Add the watercress to the potato mixture, stirring for 30 seconds or until wilted. Process in batches in a blender until puréed. Add the desired amount of reserved cream and mix well. Stir in the lemon juice, salt and pepper.

Serves 10

■

I try to stress the importance of following one's dreams and always believe in yourself. Nothing comes easily; however, with hard work and determination, anything is possible. I feel that women of my generation and ones to follow have incredible opportunities in having interesting and challenging work, coupled with a loving and strong family life. We all must work at having a balanced lifestyle and take time out to enjoy friends and relax.

Port Clyde Broccoli Salad Sandwich

■ ■ ■ ■ ■

1 cup finely chopped broccoli florets
1 teaspoon (or less) mayonnaise
Juice from 1 lemon wedge
Salt and pepper to taste
2 slices bread

*M*ix the broccoli with just enough mayonnaise to bind in a bowl. Add the lemon juice, salt and pepper and mix well. Spread on 1 slice of the bread; top with the remaining bread slice.

Serves 1

Peter Simon

Judy Blume

Selling more than sixty million copies of her books, Judy Blume is one of America's most popular authors of fiction for young people. To date, she has written twenty-one books, including such recognizable titles as Are You There God? It's Me, Margaret; Superfudge; Blubber; *and* Just as Long As We're Together. *Judy Blume has won more than ninety awards in thirty states and around the world, including the "Children's Choice" Award.*

■

Learn you can think for yourself. And thinking for yourself will be the single most important part of the rest of your life. That means recognizing your options, weighing the pros and cons, learning to make wise decisions, taking responsibility for your own actions. It also means being aware of other people's feelings. Okay, so you'll make some mistakes along the way. We all do. But at least they'll be your mistakes. And you'll learn from them, too.

Susan McGee Bailey

A Girl Scout through high school and troop leader in Taipei, Taiwan, Susan McGee Bailey is the Director of the Center for Research on Women and of the Stone Center at Wellesley College in Massachusetts. These two prestigious centers are devoted to studying and improving the lives of women and girls. As a result of her travels to Bejing for the fourth World Conference on Women, she is currently working on curriculum for middle school boys and girls on the ways girls and women around the world are working to improve life for everyone.

Three-Bean Salad

■ ■ ■ ■ ■

1 (16-ounce) can cut green beans, drained
1 (16-ounce) can yellow wax beans, drained
1 (16-ounce) can red kidney beans, drained
1 green bell pepper, finely chopped
$^1/_2$ cup finely chopped onion
$^1/_2$ cup vegetable oil
$^1/_2$ cup cider vinegar
$^1/_2$ cup sugar
1 teaspoon salt
$^1/_2$ teaspoon pepper

*C*ombine the green beans, yellow wax beans, kidney beans, green pepper and onion in a bowl and mix gently. Combine the oil, vinegar, sugar, salt and pepper in a bowl and mix well. Pour over the bean mixture, tossing gently to coat. Chill, covered, until serving time. Drain as desired before serving. Flavor is enhanced if prepared 2 to 24 hours in advance.

Serves 5

■

I believe that some of the most valuable and interesting learning comes from doing things that may seem, at first, too difficult and scary. It is important to take risks, to try again if your first attempt fails. Try always to keep in mind what you think and what you care about, rather than what you think others may think you should think! And finally, to remember that advice like this is easy to give but hard to do!

Gran Salad

■ ■ ■ ■ ■

1 (3-ounce) package lime gelatin
1 cup boiling water
3 ounces cream cheese, softened
1 (8-ounce) can crushed pineapple
³/₄ cup chopped pecans
1 envelope whipped topping mix, prepared

Dissolve the gelatin in the boiling water in a bowl and mix well. Add the cream cheese, beating until blended. Let stand until cool. Stir in the undrained pineapple, pecans and whipped topping. Spoon into a rectangular dish. Chill until set. Cut into squares to serve. May substitute 8 ounces whipped cream or 8 ounces whipped topping for the whipped topping mix.

Serves 6

■

Blend education, ambition, persistence and dedication. Mix humor and love with compassion and tolerance. Top with honesty, confidence and pride. Share with your family first. Be spiritually strong and always strive to "give something back."

Dr. Brenda R. Williams

The Associate Provost at the University of New Haven, Dr. Brenda R. Williams is an educator whose experience includes twenty-five years in the field of education. During this tenure, she has served as professor and administrator at the University of Hartford, and lectured on the topics of gender equity in higher education and African-American Literature. Dr. Williams serves on numerous boards and is a member of several professional organizations, including the Board of Directors of the Connecticut Humanities Council, the National Congress of Black Faculty, and Connecticut Women in Higher Education. Listed in "Who's Who Among America's Teachers," she has received many honors and awards for her achievements, including an invitation as Keynote speaker by the National Council of Negro Women.

CAPITAL CITIES/ABC, INC.

Joan Lunden

Co-host of ABC News' "Good Morning America" since 1980, Joan Lunden is one of television's most versatile reporters and the longest-running co-host on early morning television. She has covered a multitude of major events, including the inaugurations of three presidents, the Olympics and the 50th anniversary of VE (Victory in Europe) Day. Ms. Lunden has become one of the most visible women in the country since she joined "Good Morning America." An Entertainment Weekly *magazine poll named her "television's favorite morning anchor." And in her spare time, she has climbed and rappelled Alaska's famed Mendenhall Glacier, bungee-jumped off a 143-foot bridge, and has been at the controls of an F-18 jet and soared with the Air Force Thunderbirds.*

Curried Chicken Salad with Mangoes

■ ■ ■ ■ ■

1½ pounds boneless skinless chicken breasts
2 mangoes, peeled, cut into 1-inch pieces
2 ribs celery, chopped
4 scallions, thinly sliced (use only white bulb and part of green)
2 tablespoons fresh lime juice
¼ cup plain nonfat yogurt
¼ cup low-fat mayonnaise
1½ teaspoons curry powder
½ teaspoon cumin
Salt and pepper to taste
2 tablespoons chopped cashews (optional)

Rinse the chicken. Combine the chicken with enough water to cover in a saucepan. Remove the chicken. Bring the water to a boil. Return the chicken to the saucepan. Simmer for 5 minutes. Remove from heat. Let stand, covered, for 10 minutes. Check the chicken to make sure it is cooked through. Simmer an additional 2 minutes if needed. Chop the chicken. Combine the chicken, mangoes, celery, scallions and lime juice in a bowl and mix well. Whisk the yogurt, mayonnaise, curry powder, cumin, salt and pepper in a bowl and mix well. Add to the chicken mixture, tossing to coat. Spoon onto lettuce-lined plates. Top each serving with 2 teaspoons chopped cashews. May substitute papayas or a combination of papayas and mangoes for the mangoes.

Serves 3

Pang Pang Chicken Salad

■ ■ ■ ■ ■

2 cups shredded cooked chicken
1 cup shredded cucumber
1 tablespoon peanut butter
2 teaspoons sesame seed oil
1 teaspoon soy sauce
$^1/_2$ teaspoon sugar
$^1/_2$ teaspoon vinegar
$^1/_2$ teaspoon chili oil
$^1/_2$ teaspoon minced garlic
$^1/_2$ teaspoon minced gingerroot
$^1/_4$ teaspoon salt
Sesame seeds to taste (optional)

*C*ombine the chicken and cucumber in a bowl and mix well. Combine the peanut butter, sesame seed oil, soy sauce, sugar, vinegar, chili oil, garlic, gingerroot and salt in a bowl and mix well. Add to the chicken mixture, tossing to coat. Sprinkle with sesame seeds.

Serves 4

Cecilia Chung

Introducing a new style of cuisine to this side of the world, Cecilia Chung has opened people's minds to new ideas and new flavors. Born to a theatrical family in Shanghai, she opened China House with her husband Joseph in 1981. Through China House, Cecilia opened people's eyes and mouths to dishes that had been unknown to most Westerners. As a further challenge, Cecilia Chung opened the China House Bistro, giving Chinese culinary arts a new image in our ever-demanding, multicultural society.

■

To know what you know, and to know what you don't know, that is knowing.

Anne Gingrass

At the young age of fifteen, Anne Gingrass began her culinary career at her mother's catering business in Stamford, Connecticut. After meeting her future husband at the Culinary Institute where she studied, she and her husband David eventually developed a strong relationship with Wolfgang Puck and worked at Spago for three years. The team then went on to become managers of Postrio, earning several awards and rave reviews. In 1994, after eleven years with Wolfgang Puck, the couple opened their first solo restaurant, Hawthorne Lane, in San Francisco.

Summer Tomato Salad

■ ■ ■ ■ ■

4 slices sourdough bread
2 tablespoons virgin olive oil
1 clove of garlic
3 pounds (assorted varieties and colors) tomatoes, sliced
Herb Dressing
1/2 pint cherry tomatoes, stems removed

*B*rush bread slices on both sides with olive oil. Place on a baking sheet. Toast on both sides in a moderate oven. Rub lightly with garlic. Place the garlic croutons on a serving platter; stack with tomato slices. Drizzle the Herb Dressing over and around the tomato slices. Arrange the cherry tomatoes around the croutons.

Herb Dressing

1 each salted anchovy
1/2 clove of garlic
1/2 cup virgin olive oil
2 tablespoons each finely chopped fresh parsley, chervil, chives and basil
Salt and pepper to taste

*C*over the anchovy with water in a bowl and soak for 30 minutes; drain and rinse. Pound the anchovy and garlic in a mortar with a pestle until smooth. Mix with olive oil, herbs, salt and pepper in a small bowl.

Serves 8

Setting A New Course

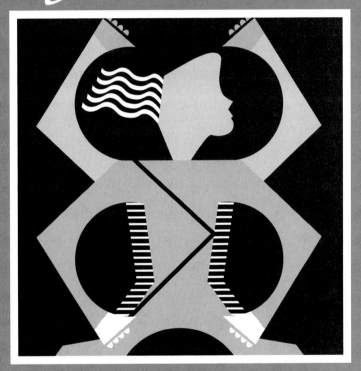

*Truth telling, innovation, creativity, perseverance,
and tenacity. . . all are ingredients women use to build
new paradigms throughout family, community, and business.*

Donna Nordin

Donna Nordin, an influential chef in contemporary Southwestern Arizona, was once mainly associated with French cuisine in the San Francisco Bay area. For years she had her own cooking school, La Grande Bouffe, and taught cooking classes across the country. In the early 1980s Donna moved to Tucson, Arizona, and in 1986 opened Cafe Terra Cotta, which continues to be the most popular restaurant in Tucson today. In 1992 she and her husband opened Cafe Terra Cotta in Scottsdale, Arizona, and most recently they opened Trio Bistro/Bar in Tucson. In 1994 Donna was inducted into the Arizona Culinary Hall of Fame.

■

Stick to your goals and always be honest with everyone along the way.

Beef Tenderloin

■ ■ ■ ■ ■

8 blue corn tortillas, cut into strips   Vegetable oil
1 (2-pound) beef tenderloin (center or end cut)
8 portobello mushrooms   16 green onions
Salt and pepper to taste

*F*ry the tortilla strips in 1 inch hot oil in a deep skillet until crispy; drain on paper towels. Grill the tenderloin over medium coals on a covered grill for 15 to 24 minutes to 160 degrees (for medium) or 170 degrees (for well done) on a meat thermometer; turn halfway through cooking. Remove from heat; let stand for 5 to 10 minutes. Brush mushrooms and green onions with oil. Grill until tender. Season with salt and pepper. Slice the mushrooms. Slice the tenderloin into 24 slices, $1/4$ to $3/8$ inch thick. Spoon Roast Tomatillo Sauce onto 8 warmed serving plates. Arrange tortilla strips in the center, 3 slices of tenderloin around the tortillas and the grilled green onions and mushrooms around the tenderloin. Serve with corn salsa.

Roast Tomatillo Sauce

15 tomatillos, husks removed   1 onion, chopped
2 teaspoons olive oil   6 chipotle chile peppers, seeded
$1/2$ cup (or more) chicken stock   1 bunch cilantro
Salt and pepper to taste

*B*rown tomatillos in a cast-iron skillet over medium-high heat, turning frequently. Remove and cool. Sauté the onion in oil in a skillet over medium heat for 5 minutes. Add tomatillos, peppers and stock. Simmer for 10 minutes. Pour into a blender; add the cilantro. Purée. Season with salt and pepper. Return to the skillet. Keep warm, covered, until serving time.

Serves 8

Nina's Beef Stew

■ ■ ■ ■ ■

3 pounds lean stew meat
1 (28-ounce) can whole tomatoes
1 (15-ounce) can tomato sauce
1 onion, chopped
3 carrots, chopped
3 potatoes, peeled and cut into quarters
1 clove of garlic, chopped
Dash of Worcestershire sauce
Dash of lemon juice
1 bay leaf
1 cup red wine
Fresh dill, salt and pepper to taste

*C*ombine the stew meat, undrained tomatoes, tomato sauce, onion, carrots, potatoes, garlic, Worcestershire sauce, lemon juice, bay leaf and wine in a large Dutch oven; mix well. Season with dill, salt and pepper. Bake, covered, at 250 degrees for 5 hours, stirring occasionally. Remove the bay leaf. Ladle into soup bowls and top with dill. May add any additional vegetables desired.

Serves 6

Murray Bognovitz

Nina Totenberg

An award-winning legal affairs correspondent for National Public Radio, Nina Totenberg's reports air regularly on NPR's critically-acclaimed news magazines "All Things Considered," "Morning Edition," and "Weekend Edition." She has won widespread recognition for her coverage of the Supreme Court and legal affairs.

■

Never spend more than one hour in the kitchen unless you love it.

Dr. Evelyn P. Fancher

Currently a Kelly Miller Smith Research Librarian at Vanderbilt University, Dr. Evelyn P. Fancher played a major role in the merger of the libraries at Tennessee State University and the University of Tennessee at Nashville. She has served as President of the Tennessee Library Association and Chair of its College Division, Chair of the Tennessee Board of Regents Librarians Council, on-site consultant for Swaziland, Africa's Agricultural Libraries, and was appointed by the Tennessee Secretary of State to serve two consecutive terms on the Tennessee Long Range Planning Committee for Libraries. Volunteering in several civic organizations, including serving as a Girl Scout leader for six years, Evelyn Fancher received the Mary Catherine Strobel Award as "Volunteer of the Year" in 1992, and was honored as "Volunteer of the Week" by the Community Resource Center in 1992.

1-2-3 Stew

■ ■ ■ ■ ■

2 to 3 pounds round steak, cubed
1 (10-ounce) can cream of mushroom soup
1 envelope onion soup mix

*P*lace the round steak in a heavy baking dish. Combine the mushroom soup and onion soup mix in a small bowl; mix well. Do not add water. Pour over the steak. Bake, covered, at 300 degrees for 3 hours. Serve over rice.

Serves 4

■

Each stage of life has its own rewards. Enjoy being a girl; enjoy young womanhood; don't rush into experiences that should be saved for true love and marriage. Finally, develop a high sense of "self-worth" and character and you will fulfill your dreams.

Phyllis Diller's Tamale Pie

■ ■ ■ ■ ■

1 pound ground beef
1 onion, chopped
1 teaspoon salt
2 tablespoons chili powder
1 (15-ounce) can whole tomatoes, or
2 (6-ounce) cans tomato sauce
1 (3-ounce) can pitted black olives, cut into halves
1 (11-ounce) can whole kernel corn
1/2 to 3/4 cup cornmeal
1/2 cup shredded Longhorn cheese
2 strips bacon

*B*rown the ground beef with onion, salt and chili powder in a large skillet, stirring until the ground beef is crumbly; drain. Stir in the tomatoes, olives, corn, cornmeal and cheese. Spoon into a baking dish. Top with the bacon. Bake at 350 degrees for 35 minutes. Recipe may be doubled.

Serves 8

Phyllis Diller

Phyllis Diller, an irrepressible lady with the outrageous laugh, is recognized as perhaps the leading female stand-up comic in the world today. She has starred on television, in movies and on stage and has headlined in venues around the world as a professional comic. A "late bloomer," she started her career at the age of 37. At the time she was a working mother of five who, urged by her husband Sherwood Diller, performed her first nightclub act in 1955. She now enters her fifth decade in show business. Phyllis is also a dedicated philanthropist, author of four books, talented piano soloist (appearing with over 100 symphonies between 1972 and 1982) and award-winning business woman.

■

Life is a do-it-yourself kit. Believe in yourself. What magical words! Tell yourself how wonderful you are and believe it. It's preventive medicine.

Dr. Joyce Brothers

America's favorite psychologist, Dr. Joyce Brothers has helped millions of people discover their own thoughts and feelings as well as provided them with insights into the thoughts and feelings of others. She broadcasts on the NBC Radio Network Monday through Fridays, is a regular columnist for Good Housekeeping *magazine, and writes a daily syndicated column published in more than 350 newspapers worldwide. From her many magazine articles and numerous television and radio appearances, she has positioned herself as one of the "most admired women" on the George Gallup poll for the past six years.*

■

Taste everything on the table—in life try as many non-dangerous new things. You never know what new directions your life will take.

Meat Loaf

■ ■ ■ ■ ■

2 eggs
2 pounds ground chuck or ground round
2 cups fresh bread crumbs
$^3/_4$ cup minced onion
$^1/_4$ cup minced green bell pepper
2 tablespoons prepared horseradish
$2^1/_2$ teaspoons salt
1 teaspoon dry mustard
$^1/_4$ cup milk or evaporated milk
$^3/_4$ cup catsup

*B*eat the eggs with a fork in a large bowl. Add the ground chuck, bread crumbs, onion and green pepper, mixing well. Stir in the horseradish, salt, mustard, milk and $^1/_4$ cup of the catsup. Shape into an oval loaf. Place in a baking dish. Spread the remaining $^1/_2$ cup catsup over the top. Bake at 400 degrees for 50 minutes.

Serves 8

Venison and Wild Rice Casserole

(Waawaashkeshiwi-wiyaas idash Manoomin)

■ ■ ■ ■ ■

1 pound venison, cubed
1 onion, chopped
2 ribs celery, chopped
8 mushrooms, chopped
1 cup wild rice
2¼ cups water
Salt to taste
1 cup blueberries, or ½ cup raisins

*B*rown the venison, onion, celery and mushrooms in a large heavy skillet. Rinse the wild rice twice in cold water; drain. Place the rice in a Dutch oven with 2¼ cups water. Add the venison mixture and season with salt. Top with the blueberries. Bake, covered, at 350 degrees for 1 hour.

Serves 4

Winona LaDuke

In addition to serving as Program Director of the Seventh Generation Fund's Environmental Program, a national Native American grant-making and advocacy organization, Winona LaDuke is also the Campaign Director of the White Earth Land Recovery Project, a reservation-based land acquisition, environment advocacy, and cultural organization. Winner of the 1988 Reebok Human Rights Award, she is a longtime environmental and indigenous rights activist, has acted as representative on many U.N. and Congressional forums and is a member of the Mississippi Band of Chippewa of the White Earth Reservation.

■

Treat all life with respect and thanks. Speak with courage and honesty. Deliberate carefully and make your decisions based on the impact on the seventh generation from now.

Jessye Norman

One of the world's most beloved singers, Jessye Norman performs in the leading opera houses and concert halls worldwide, and in truly extra-ordinary places. She sang at the opening ceremony of the Centennial Olympic Games in Atlanta, in a stadium of 85,000 and before a television viewing audience of several billion. Her work has been described by the New York Times as "repre-senting all that is virtuous in singing." Miss Norman, a lifetime member of Girl Scouts of the U.S.A., has been awarded many accolades including several Grammy Awards, many honorary doctorate degrees, the Legion of Honor and honorary Ambassadorship to the United Nations. France has named an orchid for her, and in her hometown of Augusta, Georgia, the amphitheatre and plaza overlooking the tranquil Savannah River bear her name.

■

Follow your bliss, your passion, that, without which, your life would be ordinary.

Jessye Norman's Corsican Chicken

■ ■ ■ ■ ■

6 ounces dried apricots (about 1 cup)
¹/2 cup sultana raisins
1 cup dry white wine
2 (3-pound) free-range chickens, cut into serving pieces
¹/2 cup olive oil   1 cup chopped shallots
1 small green bell pepper, julienned
2 cloves of garlic, crushed
1 tablespoon grated lemon peel
¹/2 teaspoon ground coriander   3 cups chicken broth
1 tablespoon crushed drained green peppercorns
Salt to taste
1¹/2 to 2 tablespoons cornstarch (optional)
2 tablespoons chopped fresh cilantro
4 ounces slivered almonds (about ¹/2 cup)
¹/2 cup shredded unsweetened coconut

*M*arinate apricots and raisins in wine overnight. Rinse the chicken and pat dry; discard fat and skin. Sauté the chicken in olive oil in a large heavy skillet over medium heat until browned; drain. Sauté the shallots, green pepper and garlic for 10 minutes. Arrange the chicken legs and thighs in a large baking dish; top with the sautéed vegetables. Add undrained fruit, lemon peel and coriander. Pour broth over the top. Add peppercorns and salt. Bake at 375 degrees for 25 minutes. Add the remaining chicken pieces and additional broth if necessary. Bake for 20 minutes longer or until chicken is cooked through. Thicken sauce by stirring in mixture of ¹/2 cup cooking liquid and cornstarch. Add cilantro, almonds and coconut. Bake for 10 minutes or until the coconut is browned.

Serves 8

Chicken Adobo
(Adobong Manok)

■ ■ ■ ■ ■

1 (3-pound) chicken, cut into serving pieces
$^1/_4$ cup soy sauce
$^3/_4$ cup white vinegar
1 to 2 heads of garlic, crushed
2 bay leaves
$^1/_2$ tablespoon peppercorns
Salt to taste

Rinse the chicken and pat dry. Place in a large saucepan with just enough water to cover. Add the soy sauce, vinegar, garlic, bay leaves and peppercorns. Bring to a boil; reduce the heat. Simmer for 1 hour. Remove the chicken and place on a broiler rack; reserve the cooking liquid. Broil until browned on each side. Bring the reserved cooking liquid to a boil. Cook until reduced by half. Season with salt. Arrange the chicken on a serving plate. Cover with the sauce.

Serves 6

Recipe courtesy of Reynaldo Alejandro

Loida Nicolas Lewis

Current Chairman and CEO of TLC Beatrice International Holdings, Inc., a multinational food company with sales in 1995 of $2.1 billion, Loida Nicolas Lewis is an attorney by profession. She was named by Working Woman *magazine as the top business woman in the country for 1995 and "manager to watch" by* BusinessWeek *for 1995. Mrs. Lewis is the first Asian woman to pass the New York State bar exam without having studied law in the U.S., and is one of the founders of the Asian-American Defense fund. She has spoken to audiences around the world, and also promotes the biography of her late husband.*

■

Set your Goals. Obey an inner code of conduct. Be Determined. Goals—G. Obedience—O. Determination—D. With GOD, everything is possible.

*Susan Feniger and
Mary Sue Milliken*

Making their mark on California's
culinary landscape 15 years ago with
the opening of CITY, Susan Feniger
and Mary Sue Milliken have not
slowed down since. In 1988, they
were the first women to receive the
California Restaurant Writer's
prestigious Chef of the Year Award,
and in 1993, they were two of only
sixteen chefs worldwide to be invited
to cook with Julia Child in her PBS
series, "Home Cooking with Master
Chefs." The pair own Border Grill
and host their own popular nightly
television show, "Too Hot Tamales,"
which airs on the Television Food
Network and was named "One of the
50 Great Things About Television
Now" by TV Guide. Their radio show,
"Good Food," was recently nominated
for a James Beard Award for Best
Radio Cooking Show.

*Take time to play, have fun and
be whimsical. You have the rest of
your life to be serious.*

Green Chicken Chilaquiles

■ ■ ■ ■ ■

2 whole chicken breasts, split
Salt and freshly ground pepper to taste
2 cups chicken stock   3^1/$_2$ cups Tomatillo Salsa
^{1}/$_2$ cup whipping cream   1 teaspoon salt
^{1}/$_2$ teaspoon pepper   1 onion, very thinly sliced
12 dried corn tortillas ^{1}/$_2$ cup vegetable oil
1 cup each shredded Manchego and Panela cheeses
^{1}/$_2$ cup shredded Añejo cheese

*R*inse the chicken and pat dry. Season with salt and pepper.
Cook in simmering stock in a saucepan, covered, for 15
minutes. Remove, cool and shred. Mix Tomatillo Salsa, cream,
salt, pepper, onion and chicken in a large bowl. Freshen the
tortillas in the oil in a skillet over medium-low heat for 5
seconds on each side; drain. Spread a thin layer of mixed cheeses
in a buttered 4-quart baking dish. Drain liquid from the chicken
mixture into a shallow bowl. Dip tortillas into the liquid.
Alternate layers of 4 tortillas, chicken mixture and cheese in
baking dish. Bake, covered with foil, at 350 degrees for 30
minutes. Let stand for 30 minutes.

Tomatillo Salsa

1 pound tomatillos, husked, cut into fourths
2 to 4 large jalapeños, seeded and chopped
^{1}/$_2$ cup water ^{1}/$_2$ medium onion, cut into halves
2 bunches cilantro   2 teaspoons salt

*P*rocess the first 3 ingredients in a food processor fitted
with a metal blade until chunky. Add the onion, cilantro
and salt. Process for 2 minutes. Chill, covered, for up to 3 days.

Serves 8

West African Groundnut Stew

■ ■ ■ ■ ■

1 (3-pound) chicken, skinned, cut into serving pieces
2 tablespoons peanut or canola oil
2 cups chopped onions
$^1/_2$ teaspoon cayenne pepper
1 teaspoon chopped garlic
2 cups chopped cabbage
3 cups cubed sweet potatoes or yams
3 cups tomato juice
1 cup apple juice   1 teaspoon salt
1 teaspoon peeled, grated gingerroot
1 cup chopped tomatoes
1 tablespoon chopped cilantro (optional)
$1^1/_2$ to 2 cups chopped okra (optional)
$^1/_2$ to $^3/_4$ cup freshly ground (or prepared) peanut butter

Rinse the chicken and pat dry. Brown in 1 tablespoon of the oil in a large heavy saucepan; remove and set aside. Sauté the onions in the remaining oil for 10 minutes or until soft but not browned. Stir in the cayenne and garlic. Sauté for 2 to 3 minutes longer. Add the cabbage and sweet potatoes. Cook, covered, for 1 to 2 minutes or until the cabbage begins to wilt. Stir in the tomato juice, apple juice, salt, ginger, tomatoes and cilantro. Simmer, covered, for 15 minutes or until the potatoes are tender. Add the okra. Simmer for 5 minutes longer. Stir in the peanut butter and add the chicken pieces. Simmer for 30 minutes or until the chicken is cooked through, adding additional juice or water if necessary. Serve with rice, millet or couscous. Garnish with sliced papayas, mangos, bananas or grated coconut.

Serves 8

Don West

Judy Richardson

A critically-acclaimed film producer and civil rights advocate, Judy Richardson has been associated since 1979 with the PBS documentary "Eyes on the Prize," a definitive series on the Civil Rights Movement produced by Blackside, Inc. Ms. Richardson has most recently served as the Series Associate Producer for "Eyes II" and as researcher and content advisor for "Eyes I." The 2$^1/_2$-hour documentary "Malcolm X: Make it Plain," for which she served as co-producer, was the recipient of both an Emmy and a Peabody Award. The film aired nationally on PBS' "The American Experience" and is now available on home video.

■

Surround yourself with positive people who want to do something with their lives. Find out what brings you joy and strength (music, poetry, friends, and spirituality) and try to keep these things in your life. And work in whatever ways possible for you, for a more just society.

Christine Todd Whitman

The first woman to be elected
Governor of New Jersey, Christine
Todd Whitman carries on a long
tradition of public service. Governor
Whitman was appointed by the
former governor to serve as President
of the New Jersey Board of Public
Utilities, has served on the National
Council on Crime and Delinquency
and has taught English as a second
language with her husband in New
York. She is a wife and mother of two
teenage children.

■

*Recipe for success: Start with the
love of a supportive family; add some
good education; and mix with lots of hard
work, plenty of good fortune, an
abundance of patience, and loads of
self-confidence in your own talents and
abilities. Once you have all these in the
proper proportions, all you need is
the fire of determination, and you should
be well on your way to enjoying the
sweet taste of success.*

Raspberry Chicken

■ ■ ■ ■ ■

3 cups raspberries
¹⁄₃ cup light corn syrup
2 tablespoons lemon juice
1 tablespoon cornstarch
¹⁄₂ teaspoon salt
¹⁄₁₆ teaspoon pepper
3 whole chicken breasts, split, skinned and boned

*P*rocess 2 cups of the raspberries, the corn syrup and
lemon juice in a blender at high speed until smooth; set
aside. Combine the cornstarch, salt and pepper in a small
saucepan. Add the raspberry mixture, stirring until smooth.
Bring to a boil. Cook for 1 minute, stirring constantly. Rinse the
chicken and pat dry. Place in a greased 6x10-inch baking dish.
Top with the remaining raspberries; pour the sauce over the
chicken. Bake at 400 degrees for 25 to 35 minutes or until the
chicken is cooked through.

Serves 6

Chicken with Cashew Nuts

■ ■ ■ ■ ■

This recipe has been an outstanding favorite at our family's Cambridge restaurant for as long as I can remember. There, the cashews are deep-fried, but at home I prefer to toast them instead. This reduces the amount of oil without reducing the flavor.

1 pound chicken breast fillets

2 teaspoons cornstarch   2 teaspoons dry sherry

¹/₂ teaspoon grated peeled gingerroot

2 tablespoons dark soy sauce

2 tablespoons hoisin sauce

1 teaspoon sugar   2 tablespoons water

¹/₄ cup canola, corn or peanut oil

1 clove of garlic, crushed

1 cup whole blanched cashews, toasted

1 teaspoon sesame seed oil

Rinse the chicken and pat dry. Cut into ³/₄-inch cubes. Mix with the cornstarch, sherry and gingerroot in a bowl; set aside. Combine the soy sauce, hoisin sauce, sugar and water in a small bowl, stirring until smooth; set aside. Heat the canola oil in a wok over high heat. Add the garlic. Stir-fry for 30 seconds. Stir the chicken mixture and add to the wok. Stir-fry for 1 to 2 minutes or until the chicken is cooked through. Remove and discard the garlic; reduce the heat to medium. Add the soy sauce mixture. Cook for 1 minute, stirring constantly. Add the cashews. Stir-fry for 30 seconds. Drizzle with sesame seed oil and stir well. Serve immediately.

Serves 4

Recipe from *Helen Chen's Chinese Home Cooking*, 1994, Hearst Books. Reprinted with permission from the author.

Helen Chen

Widely acknowledged as the doyenne of Chinese cooking, Helen Chen is also Chairman and CEO of Joyce Chen Products and Keilen, Ltd., placing her in the forefront of women executives in the Housewares Industry. Coming to the United States as an infant, Helen's family settled in the Boston area, where she learned not only countless recipes and cooking techniques from her mother, but also a wealth of Chinese lore and traditions. She brings the best of both worlds to her cooking as well as her oriental cookware companies, which are considered the leaders in ethnic cookware in the U.S. Helen Chen is also a widely-acknowledged cookbook author, TV personality, and corporate spokesperson.

■

Have an open and inquiring mind. Don't be afraid to ask questions. I remember someone saying to me once, "The only stupid question is the one that's never asked."

Dr. Nadine G. Barlow

With an interest in astronomy that was sparked during a fifth grade field trip to a local planetarium, Dr. Nadine G. Barlow is currently head of the astronomy program and director of the Robinson Observatory at the University of Central Florida in Orlando. In 1992, she provided scientific support to NASA's Johnson Space Center's Lunar and Mars Exploration Programs Office. In 1993, she became a Visiting Scientist at the Lunar and Planetary Institute, and in 1995, she founded Minerva Research Enterprises, a space science research and education consulting firm.

■

You can do whatever you set your mind to.

Turkey Enchilada Casserole

■ ■ ■ ■ ■

2 cups sliced cooked turkey
3 (10-ounce) cans enchilada sauce
1½ cups chopped onion
1 (10-ounce) can cream of chicken soup
1 (4-ounce) can chopped green chiles
6 corn tortillas
1½ cups shredded Cheddar cheese

*C*ombine the turkey, 2 cans of the enchilada sauce, onion, soup and green chiles in a bowl; mix well. Cut the tortillas into strips. Line a 9-inch square baking dish with half the tortilla strips. Layer half the turkey mixture, remaining tortilla strips and half the cheese in the prepared dish. Layer the remaining turkey mixture, remaining enchilada sauce and remaining cheese over the layers. Bake at 350 degrees for 45 minutes.

Serves 9

Russian Turkey Meatball Stroganoff

■ ■ ■ ■ ■

1 pound lean ground turkey
1 egg, beaten
1/2 cup dried bread crumbs
1 tablespoon dried parsley flakes, or
2 tablespoons fresh chopped parsley
1 teaspoon salt
1/8 teaspoon pepper
1 large onion, chopped
1 tablespoon paprika
1/4 cup flour
1 cup chicken or beef broth
1 tablespoon tomato paste, or 1/4 cup tomato sauce
1 cup nonfat yogurt
1 tablespoon Worcestershire sauce
8 ounces noodles, cooked

Dr. Dawna Markova

Dr. Dawna Markova is an author and educator who is internationally known for her ground-breaking research in the fields of perception and learning. She has developed an approach to learning and communication styles that enhances the untapped capacity of the human mind. Author of such books as A Creative Process for Discovering What's Right About What's Wrong *and* The Open Mind: A Compassionate Approach to Understanding the Way People Think, Learn, and Communicate, *she also co-authored* Random Acts of Kindness. *Dr. Markova is also a board member of the Visions of a Better World Foundation at the United Nations.*

Combine the turkey, egg, bread crumbs, parsley, salt and pepper in a large bowl; mix well. Shape into meatballs. Brown the meatballs in a skillet sprayed with nonstick cooking spray; remove to a warmed plate. Add the onion to a skillet sprayed with nonstick cooking spray. Cook over medium heat for 10 minutes or until the onion is lightly browned. Add the paprika. Cook for 1 to 2 minutes longer. Stir in the flour. Cook for 3 minutes or until the flour begins to brown. Stir in the broth and the tomato paste. Cook for 5 minutes or until the sauce thickens. Reduce the heat to very low. Stir in the yogurt and Worcestershire sauce. Return the meatballs to the skillet. Simmer, covered, for 10 minutes. Spoon over cooked noodles, or serve with pasta or rice.

Serves 4

Josefina Howard

The executive chef of New York's Rosa Mexicano, Josefina Howard prepares foods that showcase authentic, classical, Mexican cuisine. She has worked hard to master her appreciation of exotic and intricate Mexican cuisine. After living in Spain for 17 years, Josefina Howard moved to New York and subsequently to Mexico, where she fine-tuned her skills. Upon her return to New York, she found that the foods she had loved so much in Mexico were not available. So, she opened a lunch cafe. Since that time, she has served as head chef at Cinco de Mayo and, in 1984, she opened Rosa Mexicano.

■

*I can sum it up in three words:
No Matter What! Find a dream of
what you most want to give to the world,
a dream that is stronger than any fear
you could ever have. Then stay loyal
to it…No Matter What!*

Stuffed Flounder Rolls
(Rollos de Lenguado)

■ ■ ■ ■ ■

8 poblano chiles, roasted, peeled
1 tablespoon oil   2 tablespoons chopped onion
¹/₂ cup chicken broth
1 cup heavy cream
1 cup Champagne
4 flounder fillets (about 2 pounds), pounded to flatten
Salt and pepper to taste
1 teaspoon lemon juice
1 small onion, finely chopped
1 small tomato, finely chopped
1 clove of garlic, finely chopped
2 tablespoons butter
6 ounces baby shrimp, finely chopped
4 ounces bay scallops, finely chopped
4 cups fish broth

Soak chiles in hot salted water for 1 hour. Drain and cut into strips. Sauté chiles with 2 tablespoons onion in oil in a skillet. Process with chicken broth in a blender. Heat the cream in a heavy saucepan until reduced by half. Stir in the chile paste. Strain into a small heavy saucepan. Add the Champagne. Heat over very low heat; do not boil. Season flounder with salt, pepper and lemon juice; set aside. Sauté 1 onion, tomato and garlic in butter in a skillet. Add the shrimp and scallops. Sauté for 5 minutes. Spoon onto flounder fillets. Roll up, securing with wooden picks. Place in the simmering fish broth in a large saucepan. Cook for 5 minutes. Remove to serving plates. Spoon the chile sauce around the roll-ups.

Serves 4

Mint and Basil Marinated Salmon

■ ■ ■ ■ ■

Zest of $\frac{1}{2}$ lemon
3 tablespoons each chopped mint and basil
4 (4-ounce) salmon fillets   3$\frac{1}{2}$ tablespoons vegetable oil
**4 ounces each asparagus, spinach, sugar snap peas
and thin green beans**
4 ounces leeks, white part only, sliced into $\frac{1}{4}$-inch rounds
1 (8-ounce) potato, peeled, cut into $\frac{1}{2}$-inch cubes
1 cup heavy cream
Salt and freshly ground pepper to taste
Juice of 1 lemon   1 teaspoon chopped garlic
1 tablespoon chopped shallots
$\frac{1}{4}$ cup toasted bread crumbs   4 mint sprigs

*T*oss lemon zest with 2 tablespoons each of the mint and basil. Brush salmon with 1 tablespoon oil; rub with the mint mixture. Marinate for 1 hour in the refrigerator. Slice asparagus $\frac{1}{2}$ inch diagonally; coarsely chop spinach. Blanch the asparagus, spinach, peas and green beans separately; plunge immediately into ice water and drain. Blanch the leeks and potato; shock in ice water and drain well. Reserve 12 peas for garnish. Toss the remaining peas with the vegetables, remaining herbs, cream, salt, pepper and half the lemon juice in a large bowl. Spread a 1-inch layer of the vegetables in a gratin dish. Sweat the garlic and shallots in $\frac{1}{2}$ teaspoon oil until tender but not browned. Toss with bread crumbs, salt and pepper. Sprinkle over the vegetables. Bake at 325 degrees for 20 minutes. Season the salmon. Sear in remaining oil skin side up in a large heavy skillet until golden brown. Turn and reduce heat to medium. Cook until the salmon flakes easily. Place the salmon on a bed of vegetables. Drizzle with remaining lemon juice. Garnish with the reserved peas and mint sprigs.

Serves 4

Jody Adams

Mark Ostow Photography

With a menu inspired by her travels through France, Italy, and Spain, chef Jody Adams opened Rialto in September of 1994, after forming a partnership with three others. Four months after the restaurant's opening, the Boston Globe *awarded Rialto four stars, its highest rating. Beginning her culinary career in Boston in 1983, Jody worked as sous chef at Hamersley's Bistro and as executive chef of Michela's. Among her awards, she was given the "Best Chef de Cuisine" award from* Boston Magazine *in 1991, and has been nominated for the James Beard award for Best Chef of the Northeast for three years in a row.*

■

*The three most important things you
need to ensure your success are: one,
to choose a career in a field that you love;
two, be assertive in asking for what you
need; and three, surround yourself with
people who support you and share in
your vision for yourself.*

Joyce Goldstein

Founder and director of California Street Cooking School, San Francisco's first International Cooking School, Joyce Esersky Goldstein has been a teacher, a kitchen architect, a restaurant owner, restaurant critic and chef. She is the recipient of the 1993 James Beard Perrier Jouët Award for best chef in California, on the founding Board of Directors International Association of Women Chefs & Restaurateurs, and on the boards of several philanthropic organizations and projects. She was an owner and chef of Square One Restaurant in San Francisco and is currently a leading food consultant.

Take risks. Challenge authority. Pursue your passions and learn from "failure" because often a disappointment opens the door to success.

Salmon Wrapped in Grape Leaves

You might be surprised to learn how many countries have variations of this recipe in their national repertoire. Spain, Italy, Greece and Turkey consider this part of their cuisine, and this has become a signature dish of mine.

³/₄ cup raisins
²/₃ cup olive oil
3 tablespoons lemon juice
Salt and pepper to taste
³/₄ cup chopped, peeled tomatoes or 1 cup tomato sauce
6 (6-ounce) salmon fillets
12 large grape leaves, stems removed, rinsed and patted dry
¹/₂ cup toasted pine nuts

Soak the raisins in hot water in a bowl until softened. Purée ¹/₄ cup of the raisins in a blender. Combine with the olive oil, lemon juice, salt, pepper, tomatoes, remaining raisins and a small amount of the soaking water in a small bowl; set aside. Wrap each salmon fillet in 2 grape leaves. Brush with a small amount of olive oil. Place on a rack in a broiler pan. Broil for 3 to 4 minutes on each side or until salmon flakes easily. Remove to serving plates. Spoon the raisin sauce over the fillets; top with the pine nuts. Serve with rice pilaf and sautéed spinach or grilled zucchini. May grill the salmon over medium hot coals.

Serves 6

Sesame-Crusted Swordfish

■ ■ ■ ■ ■

4 (6 to 8 ounce) swordfish steaks, 1¹/₂ inches thick
6 tablespoons mixed black and white sesame seeds
Kosher salt and freshly ground pepper to taste

*C*oat the swordfish with sesame seeds; season. Heat 1 teaspoon oil in a skillet over medium-high heat until the oil begins to smoke. Sear the steaks for 3 minutes, turn and sear for 5 minutes. Spoon Potatoes and Scallions onto warm plates. Add swordfish. Drizzle Ginger Vinaigrette over the top.

Ginger Vinaigrette

¹/₄ teaspoon kosher salt   ¹/₄ cup Champagne vinegar
9 tablespoons virgin olive oil   3 tablespoons sesame oil
1 tablespoon each minced shallots and grated ginger
¹/₂ teaspoon cracked black pepper

*W*hisk ingredients together in order listed in a bowl. Chill for 24 hours to 2 weeks.

Potatoes and Scallions

6 small purple or blue Peruvian potatoes
6 small fingerling or creamer potatoes
Kosher salt to taste   1 tablespoon sesame oil
1 bunch scallions, trimmed, diagonally sliced 1 inch thick
Freshly ground pepper to taste

*B*oil potatoes in salted water for 15 minutes; drain. Chill for 30 minutes. Slice ¹/₈ inch thick. Sauté potatoes in sesame oil with scallions for 10 minutes. Season and keep warm.

Serves 4

Debra Ponzek

One of the top chefs cooking in America today, Debra Ponzek has received accolades for her innovative Provencal-inspired cuisine. She has been selected as one of the "Ten Best New American Chefs" by Food & Wine Magazine, *and as "Rising Chef of the Year" in 1992 by the James Beard Foundation. In 1994, she published her first book entitled* American Accent: Debra Ponzek's Spirited Cuisine. *She is currently chef and proprietor of Aux Délices, Foods by Debra Ponzek, a gourmet, prepared-food shop in Greenwich, Connecticut.*

■

Follow your dreams. Life is too short to not enjoy what you're doing. Also, integrate travel into your life whenever possible—there is so much to see and learn from other cultures.

Anne Rosenzweig

Executive chef and co-owner of Arcadia in New York City and the chef-proprietor of The Lobster Club, Anne Rosenzweig is a cooking expert whose creativity and expertise have found expression in her Arcadia Seasonal Mural *and* Cookbook, *as well as numerous recipes created for national culinary publications. Selected by the White House to serve on the "Kitchen Cabinet," a panel of three chefs that advises the President and Mrs. Clinton on menus and American food, she has also lent her talents to Meals on Wheels, Share Our Strength, and Kids for Kids (for pediatric AIDS patients).*

■

Always be determined when you set your goals, and be prepared to work harder than anyone else to achieve those goals. And remember to enjoy the struggle.

Crab and Couscous Cakes

■ ■ ■ ■ ■

1 cup fish or chicken stock	2 cups Israeli couscous
2 tablespoons butter	$^{1}/_{2}$ cup vegetable oil
1 bunch scallions, minced	2 cloves garlic, minced

2 tablespoons chopped cilantro

2 tablespoons lemon juice	16 ounces crab meat
$^{1}/_{4}$ cup chopped tomatoes	$^{1}/_{4}$ cup bread crumbs
1 tablespoon Dijon mustard	1 egg, beaten
Salt and pepper to taste	1 bunch arugula, torn

Cucumber Vinaigrette

*B*ring the stock to a boil in a small saucepan. Pour over the couscous in a bowl and stir. Let stand, covered, for 5 minutes. Add butter and 2 tablespoons oil and stir to fluff. Sauté the scallions and garlic in 2 tablespoons oil for 1 minute; cool. Stir in cilantro and lemon juice. Add couscous and next 7 ingredients; mix well. Shape into 8 cakes. Brown the cakes 1 at a time in the remaining oil in a skillet. Toss arugula with the Cucumber Vinaigrette. Arrange on serving plates and top with a crab cake.

Cucumber Vinaigrette

2 large cucumbers, peeled, seeded

$^{1}/_{2}$ cup olive oil

2 tablespoons Champagne vinegar

1 tablespoon pepper   1 clove of garlic, minced

2 tablespoons fresh dill

1 teaspoon sugar   Salt to taste

*C*ombine all the ingredients in a food processor container. Process until smooth and thickened. Set aside.

Serves 8

Shrimp and Tasso with Five-Pepper Jelly

■ ■ ■ ■ ■

$^1/_8$ teaspoon each minced garlic and shallot
$^1/_2$ teaspoon butter plus $1^1/_2$ pounds butter, softened
5 ounces Crystal Hot Sauce   2 ounces heavy cream
36 jumbo shrimp, shelled and deveined
6 ounces spicy tasso, cut into 1-inch julienne strips
$^1/_2$ cup seasoned flour   Vegetable oil for frying
Five-Pepper Jelly   36 pickled okra

Sauté garlic and shallot in $^1/_2$ teaspoon butter in a small heavy saucepan. Add the Crystal Hot Sauce. Cook over medium heat until reduced by $^3/_4$. Add cream. Cook until reduced by half. Whisk in remaining softened butter 1 tablespoon at a time. Set aside. Make a $^1/_4$-inch cut in the back of each shrimp. Secure tasso strip on cut with a wooden pick. Dust shrimp with flour. Fry in hot oil in a skillet until lightly browned; drain. Toss with the cream sauce until coated. Spread the Five-Pepper Jelly on a serving plate. Top with alternating rows of shrimp and okra.

Five-Pepper Jelly

3 ounces honey   6 ounces white vinegar
1 each red, yellow and green bell pepper, chopped
1 jalapeño, chopped $^1/_4$ teaspoon pepper   Salt to taste

Cook the honey and vinegar in a nonaluminum saucepan over medium heat until reduced and very sticky. Add bell peppers, jalapeño and pepper. Cook until soft. Season with salt.

Serves 6

Ella Brennan

Consistently recognized for her fine contributions to the cooking industry, Ella Brennan and her restaurant, Commander's Palace, received the 1993 James Beard Award for Outstanding Service. The prestigious Beard Foundation also named Commander's Palace Outstanding Restaurant in 1996. Ella Brennan has been a restaurateur for over fifty years. She attests that she does not work as an individual, but as a family, with relatives from brothers and sisters to nieces and nephews running her restaurants. Ella Brennan is a member of Cook's Magazine's Who's Who of Cooking in America.

■

It is most important to get a good education in order to take care of yourself financially and emotionally. Be flexible and adaptable and always have a good sense of humor.

Steve Fenn/ABC

Robin R. Roberts

One of ESPN's most versatile commentators, Robin Roberts' assignments have included hosting Sunday morning's "Sunday SportsDay," contributing to "NFL PrimeTime," and providing reports and interviews from the field. In June, 1995, Roberts signed a new agreement into the year 2001, allowing her to host ABC Sports "Wide World of Sports" while continuing to host the 6:30 p.m. ET edition of ESPN's "SportsCenter." At the 1996 NCAA Women's Final Four, the inaugural Robin Roberts Sports Journalism Scholarship, created by the Women's Institute on Sport and Education, will be presented.

■

A dream is only a dream until you write it down on paper, then it becomes a goal. It is important to dream but even more important to do whatever is necessary to fulfill that dream.

Lemon Pepper Barbecue Shrimp

■ ■ ■ ■ ■

$^1/_2$ cup olive oil
3 cups lemon juice
2 tablespoons freshly ground pepper
12 large shrimp, peeled, deveined and split

*C*ombine the olive oil, lemon juice and pepper in a shallow glass bowl; mix well. Add the shrimp, adding additional lemon juice or oil so the marinade completely covers the shrimp. Marinate for 2 hours in the refrigerator. Remove the shrimp from the marinade. Place on a grill rack over medium coals. Grill for 3 minutes on each side or until the shrimp turn pink.

Serves 4

Thai Curry Sea Scallops

■ ■ ■ ■ ■

The galangal, turmeric and Thai chiles needed for the curry paste are available at Asian specialty stores.

5 dried Thai chiles
4 ounces fresh galangal (Thai ginger), peeled
4 ounces fresh turmeric, peeled
4 ounces fresh ginger, peeled
8 ounces shallots, peeled
1 head of garlic   1 bunch cilantro
Juice of 2 limes
$^1/_4$ cup (scant) plus 2 tablespoons peanut oil
20 large sea scallops
$^2/_3$ cup chicken stock $^1/_2$ cup coconut milk
Salt to taste

Soak the chiles in hot water to cover in a bowl until softened. Prepare a curry paste by combining the galangal, turmeric, ginger, shallots, garlic, cilantro, lime juice and chiles in a blender container. Process until finely chopped. Add $^1/_4$ cup peanut oil 1 tablespoon at a time, processing until a smooth thick paste forms; set aside. Heat 2 tablespoons of the peanut oil in a large nonstick skillet until the peanut oil begins to smoke. Remove from the heat. Add the scallops. Return to the heat. Sear the scallops for 2 to 3 minutes on each side. Remove to a warm platter; discard oil from the skillet. Add 3 tablespoons of the curry paste to the skillet. Cook until heated through, stirring frequently. Add the chicken stock. Cook until the mixture is reduced by half. Add the coconut milk and salt. Simmer until the mixture is thickened and coats the back of a spoon. Pour over the scallops and serve immediately.

Serves 4

Christine Keff

Appearing in the Burt Wolf PBS series "Great Women Chefs," Christine Keff is owner and chef of Seattle's Flying Fish Restaurant. Initially an unexpected candidate for the culinary world, with a background in mathematics and social relations, she went on to conduct her apprenticeship at the renowned Four Seasons Restaurant under the direction of Seppi Renggli. Since then, she has traveled around the country and the world, combining the experiences from her culinary travels with her love of the Northwest. She has been honored by Pacific Northwest Magazine *as Seattle's Best Chef in 1993. Her current venture, Flying Fish, was recently named by* Bon Appetit *as "one of the top 14 new restaurants across the country."*

■

Follow your heart in life. Be strong, be tough, but don't forget to listen to the voice inside.

Barbara Lazaroff

A restaurateur and architectural designer, Barbara Lazaroff is renowned for her innovative restaurant concepts. As president of Imaginings Interior Design, Inc., she has designed popular restaurants such as Spago, Chinois, Granita and Postrio and the Wolfgang Puck Cafes. Lazaroff also owns and operates these restaurants, with her husband, Wolfgang Puck. In 1995, she received the DuPont Antron Award for her carpet designed exclusively for the Cafes, and she and her husband received the Silver Spoon Award by Food Arts magazine as well as the 1994 James Beard Humanitarian of the Year Award for their work with "Meals on Wheels."

Along this road I have never forgotten that in life as well as in the business world, women are a sisterhood. One woman's success is every woman's success...and we are all strengthened when we extend our hand and help another young woman along the path.

Barbara's "Stay Fit" Angel Hair Pasta with Tomato, Basil and Garlic Sauce and Grilled Shrimp

1 small onion, minced
2 cloves of garlic, minced
1 pound plum tomatoes, cored, seeded, chopped
1 cup chicken stock
6 to 8 basil leaves, julienned
Salt and freshly ground pepper to taste
8 ounces fresh angel hair pasta
6 ounces fresh shrimp, peeled, deveined
Grated Parmesan cheese to taste
1 tablespoon chopped fresh basil

Sauté the onion in a nonstick saucepan over medium heat for 4 to 5 minutes or until slightly tender. Add the garlic. Sauté for 1 minute longer. Add the tomatoes. Simmer for 2 to 3 minutes. Add the chicken stock. Cook for 15 to 20 minutes or until the mixture is reduced and thickened. Strain into a large saucepan. Add the basil leaves, salt and pepper. Cover to keep warm. Cook the pasta in boiling salted water until softened but not cooked through. Drain well and stir into the sauce. Cook over medium heat until the pasta is cooked to taste. Grill the shrimp for 2 minutes on each side or until cooked through. Pour the pasta into a serving bowl. Arrange the shrimp around the edge. Sprinkle with chopped basil. Add the cheese; toss lightly.

Serves 2

Penne with Corn and Uncooked Tomato Sauce

■ ■ ■ ■ ■

1¹/₂ tablespoons red wine vinegar
3 tablespoons olive oil
Salt and pepper to taste
¹/₂ cup cooked whole kernel corn
1 pound very ripe tomatoes, seeded, chopped
¹/₄ cup thinly sliced scallions
8 ounces penne or spiral pasta

Whisk the vinegar in a bowl with the oil, salt and pepper. Add the corn, tomatoes and scallions. Let stand while cooking the pasta. Cook the pasta in boiling salted water until al dente; drain well. Toss with the tomato mixture to coat. Spoon into serving bowls. Recipe may be doubled.

Serves 2

■

I just want the generation coming up to laugh a lot along the way. Up or down, love the ride. I also think women are lured by the beauty of the detail. But we can also match men as big dreamers. To ensure that we become the CEOs, we have to keep on confidently stressing the strategy and the dreams, not just the details and the tactics.

Diane Sawyer

Co-anchor of ABC News' "PrimeTime Live" and "Turning Point," Diane Sawyer has traveled extensively across the United States and abroad to report on and investigate a wide range of topics and to interview a diverse group of newsmakers and personalities. Prior to joining ABC News, Sawyer spent nine years at CBS News, including serving as co-anchor of "60 Minutes." The recipient of several John F. Kennedy Journalism Awards and National Headliner Awards, among others, she is recognized as a broadcast reporter whose interviews have made a difference in the lives of millions of people.

Judy Rodgers

Chef and owner of Zuni Café in San Francisco, Judy Rodgers has brought national acclaim to her restaurant and her brand of honest, yet sophisticated, food from the heart. As a high school exchange student in Roanne, France, she found herself at the kitchen door of the Troisgros' Family Hotel and Restaurant and learned to appreciate the art of food and cooking. After graduating from Stanford University, she worked for several years as the lunch chef at Chez Panisse, and subsequently opened the Union Hotel in Benicia, California, where she gained early renown for simple American fare. Her efforts earned her a place on the first "Who's Who in Cooking America" roster in 1984.

■

When you choose your vocation, choose what you love to do and what you know you can put your heart into.

Pasta with Beans and Pancetta

■ ■ ■ ■ ■

1 cup cannellini beans, soaked overnight
1 carrot, peeled, cut into chunks
1 rib celery, leaves removed   1 onion, cut into quarters
1 bay leaf   1 teaspoon sea salt
4 tablespoons extra-virgin olive oil
3 cups chopped Roma or other fleshy tomatoes
Salt to taste   1 medium onion, finely chopped
4 cloves of garlic, chopped
2 ounces pancetta, sliced $1/8$-inch thick, chopped
3 chile pods, chopped
1 sprig each of parsley and sage, chopped
16 ounces penne or fusilli pasta   Cracked pepper to taste

Drain and rinse the beans. Place in a large heavy stockpot. Add enough water to cover beans by 1 inch. Bring to a simmer, skimming frequently. Add the carrot, celery, onion quarters, bay leaf, 1 teaspoon sea salt and 1 teaspoon of the olive oil. Simmer until the beans are tender but not mushy, adding water as needed. Cool the beans in the cooking liquid. Toss the tomatoes with a small amount of salt. Drain in a colander. Sweat the chopped onion in the remaining olive oil with a small amount of salt in a skillet. Add the garlic. Cook over low heat; do not brown. Add the pancetta. Simmer for 5 minutes. Add the tomatoes, chili pods, parsley and sage. Simmer until thickened and the flavors merge, stirring occasionally. Drain the beans, discarding the bay leaf. Add to the tomato sauce. Simmer while the pasta is cooking. Cook the pasta in lightly salted boiling water; drain well. Combine with the sauce mixture, tossing to coat. Season with cracked pepper. Garnish with grated Pecorino Romano cheese.

Serves 6

Tomato Basil Pasta

■ ■ ■ ■ ■

2 pounds pasta
1 pound feta cheese, crumbled
3 cups chopped tomatoes
1 cup chopped purple onion
2 teaspoons Spike or mixture of salt and pepper
$^1/_4$ teaspoon freshly ground pepper
$^1/_2$ cup chopped fresh basil
3 cloves of garlic
$^1/_2$ cup olive oil
2 teaspoons fresh lemon juice
2 tablespoons balsamic vinegar
1 cup chopped fresh basil

*C*ook the pasta using package directions; drain well. Combine with the feta cheese, tomatoes, onion, Spike, pepper and $^1/_2$ cup basil in a large bowl, mixing well. Process the garlic, olive oil, lemon juice, vinegar and 1 cup basil in a blender until puréed. Pour over the pasta mixture, tossing to coat. May increase the oil, lemon juice and vinegar if the mixture seems dry.

Serves 8

Ladies Professional Golf Association

Michelle McGann

The winner of two Ladies Profess-ional Golf Association victories, Michelle McGann joined the LPGA in 1988 at the age of 18. By 1991, she had already recorded five top-ten finishes. Leading the Tour in driving distance, number of eagles, and total birdies in 1992, she captured her first career victory at the Sara Lee Classic in 1995. Michelle earned her second victory at the Youngstown-Warren LPGA Classic on the third hole of a sudden-death playoff.

■

"I was taught that everything is attainable if you're prepared to give up, to sacrifice, to get it. Whatever you want to do, you can do it, if you want to do it badly enough, and I do believe that." This quote from Og Mandino's book, The Greatest Miracle in The World, has provided me with the inspiration to continue on through much adversity.

Cary Hazlegrove

Sarah Leah Chase

The renowned owner of a specialty food shop and catering business on the island of Nantucket, Sarah Leah Chase has become a widely-acknowledged cookbook author as well. The name of her specialty food shop, Que Sera Sarah (which she translated loosely as "whatever will be me"), justified a menu that changed daily. With the shop's success, she decided to embark on her literary voyage and begin writing cookbooks. The co-author of the best-selling Silver Palate Good Times Cookbook, *she is the author of the* Nantucket Open House Cookbook *and* Cold Weather Cooking. *A media spokeswoman for the Butterball Turkey Talk-Line, Sarah Leah Chase also writes the food column for* The Beacon, *Nantucket's weekly newspaper.*

Tortellini with Sun-Dried Tomato Pesto

■ ■ ■ ■ ■

4 ounces pepperoni, chopped
3 tablespoons Dijon mustard
4 cloves of garlic, minced
1 tablespoon fennel seeds
1 (7-ounce) jar sun-dried tomatoes packed in oil
1¹/₂ cups olive oil
2 tablespoons fresh lemon juice
Salt and pepper to taste
2 pounds cheese or meat tortellini, cooked, drained
2 ripe tomatoes, seeded, chopped
1 yellow bell pepper, seeded, chopped
8 ounces pepperoni, thinly sliced
¹/₂ cup chopped fresh parsley
3 tablespoons chopped fresh basil

*C*ombine 4 ounces pepperoni, mustard, garlic, fennel seeds and undrained sun-dried tomatoes in a food processor container fitted with a steel blade. Process until smooth. Add the olive oil in a thin stream, processing constantly until the mixture is smooth. Season with lemon juice, salt and pepper. Combine the tortellini, tomatoes, bell pepper and 8 ounces pepperoni in a large bowl. Add the pesto, tossing to coat. Sprinkle with parsley and basil. Serve warm or at room temperature.

Serves 8

Hot Things

■ ■ ■ ■ ■

**1 small onion, finely chopped
1 cup hot pickled vegetables, drained, chopped
4 flour tortillas
8 ounces Cheddar or hot pepper jack cheese, shredded
1/2 cup sour cream
1/2 cup prepared salsa
Olive oil for frying**

*M*ix the onion and pickled vegetables in a small bowl. Spoon an equal amount onto each tortilla. Layer with equal amounts of cheese, sour cream and salsa. Roll up to enclose filling, securing with wooden picks. Heat a small amount of olive oil in a large skillet over medium heat. Add the tortilla roll-ups. Fry until golden brown. Serve with a green salad.

Serves 4

■

Follow your dream with all courage and imagination. Dare to dream a large dream. Stay in service some way. Make more beauty in the world.

Irene Young Photography

Cris Williamson

A pioneer of women's music, Cris Williamson is an ambassador of positive female imaging through music that celebrates human strength, tenacity, and the resilience of women. Through her illuminating and empowering album "The Changer and the Changed," Cris Williamson captures the beautiful strength of women and its impact on those around them, helping women find their voices. Today, 20 years later, "The Changer" still retains its power, and remains one of the best-selling independent music albums of all time and the best-selling "women's music" album in history. With a voice that is stronger and richer than ever, Williamson enjoys a status of teacher, spirit healer, and promoter of the art of the possible. Williamson is co-founder of In the Best Interests of the Children, Inc., the wholly volunteer nonprofit pediatric AIDS organization that develops entertainment-based HIV education programming, and co-sponsors Camp Colors, the family day camp for kids with HIV/AIDS, with Lasell College in Newton, Massachusetts.

Helen Gurley Brown

Helen Gurley Brown has been Editor in Chief of Cosmopolitan *magazine since 1965.* Cosmopolitan *now sells three million copies and is one of the largest-selling magazines on U.S. newsstands, with 28 foreign editions in print. Helen is a well known television personality and book publisher, whose first book, published in 1962, was entitled* Sex and the Single Girl. *Her most recent book, published in 1993, is* The Late Show, *a Semiwild but Practical Survival Plan for Women Over 50. The Magazine Publishers of America honored Helen Gurley Brown with the 1995 Henry Johnson Fisher Award. This prestigious award is the magazine publishing industry's highest honor. Mrs. Brown is the first female recipient.*

Welsh Rarebit

■ ■ ■ ■ ■

Welsh Rarebit has been a supper favorite for generations. Edwardians and Victorians made them in chafing dishes "after the theater." You make yours in a saucepan. It will taste wonderful, especially when you eat it propped up in bed.

1 tablespoon butter
1 tablespoon whole wheat flour
$1/4$ teaspoon salt
Pepper to taste
$1/2$ cup milk
4 ounces Cheddar cheese, cubed
1 English muffin, split
Paprika to taste

*M*elt the butter in a saucepan over low heat. Stir in the flour, salt and pepper. Add the milk gradually, stirring until smooth. Cook until the sauce begins to thicken. Add the cheese. Cook until the cheese is melted, stirring frequently. Toast the muffin halves. Pour the cheese mixture over the muffin halves; dust with paprika. May substitute vegetables, such as broccoli, cauliflower or zucchini, for the muffin.

Serves 1

■

Throughout your life, do the difficult or boring thing in front of you that has to be done...get it over with...the chore...after that comes the play and all the delicious rewards that will accrue from the discipline and hard work.

Making Connections

*The wisdom of women's work is often the art
of their collaboration—of connecting the best contributions
of individuals to develop a product of synergy,
where the whole is greater than the sum of its parts.*

Maria Conchita Alonso

A Grammy-nominated recording artist who has made a significant contribution to American movies, Maria Conchita Alonso recently added to her list of successes by becoming the first Latin-American-born actress to star on Broadway. While starring on Broadway as 'Aurora/Spider Woman' in Hal Prince's Kiss of the Spider Woman, Alonso simultaneously filmed the independent feature Caught, co-starring Edward James Olmos. The film received rave reviews at this year's Sundance Film Festival. Other feature film credits include Moscow on the Hudson, Colors, and Predator II, to name a few. On television, Alonso recently starred in ABC's four-hour miniseries "Texas," based on the best-selling novel by James Michener. Having recorded 10 albums, which earned her several Grammy nominations, Alonso has a musical career that has kept pace with her film work.

Cauliflower and Cheese Casserole

■ ■ ■ ■ ■

3 cups cauliflower, finely chopped
2 cups white sauce, heated
1 green bell pepper, finely chopped
1 cup thick tomato purée
Salt to taste
¹/₂ cup fine bread crumbs
1 cup softened nonfat cream cheese
2 tablespoons melted lowfat butter

*S*team the cauliflower in a steamer until tender-crisp. Combine the hot white sauce and cauliflower in a bowl and mix well. Add the green pepper, tomato purée and salt and mix well. Pour into a baking dish. Combine the bread crumbs, cream cheese and butter in a bowl and mix well. Spread over the cauliflower mixture. Bake, covered, at 350 degrees for 20 minutes. Remove the cover. Bake until brown. May substitute heated lowfat mushroom soup for the white sauce.

Serves 8

■

Fight for your beliefs—Anything is possible (but not easy) if you believe in yourself. Be persistent.

Eggplant Casserole

■ ■ ■ ■ ■

1 large eggplant
Salt to taste
1 cup shredded Swiss cheese
1 cup grated Parmesan cheese
3 medium tomatoes, sliced
Pepper to taste
¼ cup butter
½ (8-ounce) can tomato sauce
1 cup seasoned bread crumbs

*P*eel the eggplant and cut into slices. Place in a bowl with enough cold salted water to cover. Let stand for 30 minutes and drain. Grease the bottom and sides of a 9x13-inch baking dish. Mix the cheeses in a bowl, reserving ⅓ of the mixture. Layer ⅓ of the eggplant and ½ of the tomato slices in the prepared baking dish. Season with salt and pepper. Layer ½ of the remaining cheese mixture over the tomatoes. Repeat the layers. Add the remaining eggplant. Dot with the butter. Pour the tomato sauce over the top and sprinkle with the bread crumbs. Top with the reserved cheese mixture. Bake at 350 degrees for 1 hour.

Serves 12

Harry Langdon Photography

Debbie Reynolds

The star of more than 30 motion pictures, two Broadway shows, two television series, as well as dozens of television appearances, Debbie Reynolds celebrates over 45 years in show business. She was born Mary Frances Reynolds, and her career was launched when she was discovered at a beauty contest at the age of 16. Since then, she has starred in such acclaimed films as Singin' in the Rain, *one of the greatest screen musicals of all time, and* The Unsinkable Molly Brown, *for which she was nominated for an Oscar. A lifetime supporter of the Girl Scouts, Debbie Reynolds has also helped raise millions of dollars for emotionally disturbed children as founder and president of the Thalians.*

Nathalie Dupree

To millions of television viewers, Nathalie Dupree is one of America's hottest cooking sensations. She has hosted more than 300 half-hour television cooking shows, and has over 500,000 hard-back copies of her books in print. An award winning author, she is also a contributor to countless newspaper columns and the host of "Home Cooking," a show offering daily cooking and entertainment tips that is syndicated on over 800 radio stations. She is also a noted speaker and leading consultant to the food industry.

Follow your heart, regardless of the status, prestige or money a position seems to offer. I was told cooking was demeaning, low-paying and too hard for a woman, and that "Ladies didn't cook for a living". God bless Julia Child, who made it possible for ladies to cook!

Grits and Greens

■ ■ ■ ■ ■

This is a wonderful and unusual dish that can be used as a dip or as a vegetable side dish! If you have any tiny poke sallet volunteering in your yard, don't throw it away. Cook the tiny leaves and stems, but avoid the toxic berries and root.

3 cups milk   1 cup heavy cream
1 cup quick grits   6 tablespoons butter
1 pound spinach, turnip greens or poke sallet leaves, rinsed, stems discarded
1¹/₂ cups freshly grated imported Parmesan cheese
Salt and freshly ground pepper to taste
7 poke sallet stems the size of young asparagus

*C*ombine the milk and cream in a large heavy nonstick saucepan. Cook over medium heat just to the boiling point, stirring frequently. Stir in the grits. Cook over low heat for 5 to 10 minutes or until thickened, stirring frequently. Remove from the heat. Stir in 2 tablespoons of the butter. Place the greens with water clinging to the leaves in a large skillet. Cook over medium heat for 5 minutes or until wilted, adding several tablespoons of water if necessary. Drain the greens. Rinse in cold water and drain, pressing to remove the liquid. Melt the remaining 4 tablespoons butter in the skillet. Add the drained greens. Cook briefly, stirring to coat with the butter. Stir into the grits. Add the cheese, salt and pepper, stirring to mix. Cook the poke sallet stems in boiling water for 5 minutes; plunge immediately in cold water and drain. Pour the grits into a serving dish. Garnish with the poke sallet stems. May make ahead and reheat over low heat or in the microwave.

Serves 8

Southern Memories Cookbook by Nathalie Dupree. Published by Clarkson Potter, New York, 1993.

Cheese-Stuffed Potatoes

■ ■ ■ ■ ■

4 medium baked potatoes, warm
1 cup low-fat cottage cheese
4 teaspoons skim milk
2 tablespoons chopped green onions
$^1/_4$ teaspoon paprika

Slice each baked potato lengthwise into halves. Scoop out the pulp, leaving about $^1/_4$-inch-thick shells. Mix the cottage cheese, milk and green onions in a bowl. Add the potato pulp and mix well. Spoon the mixture into the potato shells. Arrange in a medium baking dish. Sprinkle with the paprika. Bake at 350 degrees for 10 to 15 minutes or until heated through. May be covered with waxed paper and microwaved on High for 5 minutes, turning $^1/_4$ turn halfway through the cooking time. May substitute 1 cup low-fat ricotta cheese for the cottage cheese.

Serves 8

Brenda J. Ponichtera, RD. Reprinted with permission from *Quick and Healthy Recipes and Ideas* (ScaleDown Publishing, Inc.).

■

Dream Big and Work Hard! Don't allow self-imposed limitations or others' imposing limitations to keep you from doing the things you dream about doing. Successful people aren't born that way; they're hard workers and goal-oriented people. Go after the Olympics, the Presidency, or any other dream you have. Very few people make it to the Olympics or become President. But, you CAN be one of those very few people.

Fitness Management Group

Jean Driscoll

A former Girl Scout, Jean Driscoll is a top-ranked wheelchair athlete who has won seven consecutive Boston Marathons (1990-1996) and holds both the course and world records in that event. Participating in the last two Paraolympic Games, she earned two Gold Medals, one Silver Medal, and two Bronze Medals. In 1991, the Women's Sports Foundation named Jean Driscoll Sportswoman of the Year.

Francesco Scavullo

Oprah Winfrey

Talk show host, philanthropist and businesswoman, Oprah Winfrey is also the Chairman of HARPO Entertainment Group in Chicago, joining Lucille Ball and Mary Pickford as the only women in film and TV to own their own television and film studios. Oprah began her broadcasting career at 19 as the youngest and the first African-American woman to anchor the news at WTVF-TV in Nashville. Since then, she has received Academy Award and Golden Globe nominations for acting, and The Oprah Winfrey Show has received 20 Emmys, five of which went to the host. The show has remained the number-one talk show for nine consecutive seasons.

Oprah's Potatoes

■ ■ ■ ■ ■

2^1/$_2$ pounds each red and Idaho potatoes
^{1}/$_2$ cup Butter Buds powder
^{1}/$_4$ cup creamy puréed horseradish
2 cups skim milk
1 cup chicken stock
^{1}/$_8$ teaspoon cayenne
1^1/$_2$ tablespoons ground pepper

$\mathcal{S}$rub the potatoes well. Cut unpeeled potatoes into halves. Place in a large saucepan with water to cover. Bring to a boil over medium heat. Reduce the heat to low. Simmer, covered, until the potatoes are very tender. Drain well. Add the Butter Buds and mash the potatoes. Add the horseradish, skim milk, chicken stock, cayenne and pepper. Mash until creamy but slightly lumpy. Spoon into a serving dish.

Serves 12

■

As I've been asked to share some words of inspiration with you, know that it is very important to dream Big dreams and work hard toward reaching your dreams. You can achieve all of your dreams through knowledge, but also know that you can only gain knowledge through education. Work hard in school and make the best grades you can. Remember that success starts with you and it can start right now. Only, you have to believe that you can succeed, believe that you can be whatever your heart desires, and you will have it. Don't ever let anyone or anything hold you back from doing your very best. Stay in school!

Stewed Rice
(Arroz Guisado Basico)

■ ■ ■ ■ ■

1 ounce salt pork, rinsed, finely chopped
2 ounces lean cured ham, rinsed, finely chopped
3 tablespoons lard   1 green bell pepper, minced
3 sweet chiles, seeded, minced   1 clove of garlic, minced
6 cilantro leaves, minced   1 onion, minced
2 tablespoons tomato sauce   6 pimento-stuffed olives
2 teaspoons capers   2 teaspoons salt
8 ounces fresh cooked shrimp or 2 (4-ounce) cans
2¼ cups uncooked rice, rinsed, drained
2¼ cups boiling water

*B*rown the salt pork and ham in a large heavy saucepan. Add the lard. Sauté over low heat for 10 minutes. Stir in the green pepper, chiles, garlic, cilantro leaves, onion, tomato sauce, olives, capers, salt and shrimp, mixing well. Add the rice. Sauté for 2 to 3 minutes. Stir in the boiling water. Cook over medium heat until all the water is absorbed. Turn the rice over with a fork from bottom to top. Cook, covered, over low heat for 30 minutes, turning from bottom to top after 15 minutes.

Serves 6

Irma Margarita "Maga" Rosselló

The First Lady of Puerto Rico, Irma Margarita "Maga" Rosselló has dedicated her life to helping children. Immediately after her husband became the Governor of Puerto Rico, she launched her first project, entitled ¡Yo Sí Puedo! (Yes I Can!). Literally and figuratively a labor of love, the program fosters self-esteem among Puerto Rico's young people, encouraging children and teens to scorn those who seek to destroy their promising lives through addiction, lawlessness, and out-of-wedlock parenthood. She has helped to reform the island's cumbersome adoption system and cut bureaucratic red tape so that battered children can be placed in foster homes more quickly.

Carol Bartz

CEO, President and Chairman of the Board for Autodesk, Inc., the fourth-largest software company in the world, Carol Bartz has grown net revenues for that company from $285 billion to over $534 billion since 1992. She has held management positions at other major high technology companies, such as Sun Microsystems, Digital Equipment and 3M Corporation. Bartz serves on several prominent boards and councils and is also a member of President Clinton's Export Council.

■

Become well-rounded and try to see things from many different perspectives by developing "a personal mosaic." This personal mosaic is built piece by piece by our observation and understanding of the styles and behaviors that work and don't work in the world of business and technology. Over time, these mosaics become very, very important for all of us.

They are one way that women can share and leverage their perspectives.

Baked Risotto with Eggplant

■ ■ ■ ■ ■

$^1/_4$ **cup dried porcini mushrooms**   **1 cup boiling water**
2$^1/_2$ pounds eggplant, sliced $^1/_4$ inch thick
6 tablespoons (about) olive oil
$^1/_4$ **cup minced onion or shallots**   **2 tablespoons butter**
3 cloves of garlic, chopped
3 cups chopped canned Italian tomatoes
$^1/_4$ **cup chopped Italian parsley**
3 tablespoons each chopped fresh oregano and basil
2 cups vegetable stock   **1$^1/_2$ cups Arborio rice**
$^2/_3$ **cup dry white wine**   **Freshly ground black pepper**
1 cup grated Parmesan cheese
10 ounces sliced mozzarella cheese

*S*oak mushrooms in boiling water for 30 minutes. Sprinkle eggplant with salt. Let stand for 15 minutes. Rinse and pat dry. Place in baking pan greased with olive oil. Brush with olive oil. Bake at 400 degrees for 7 minutes on each side; drain. Sauté onion in butter and 2 tablespoons olive oil in skillet. Add garlic. Sauté for 1 minute. Add undrained tomatoes. Drain mushrooms through paper-towel-lined sieve; reserve liquid. Chop mushrooms; add to tomato mixture. Simmer for 15 minutes. Add herbs. Cook for 2 minutes. Remove $^2/_3$ of the mixture. Simmer stock and mushroom liquid. Add rice to tomato mixture in skillet. Add wine and pepper. Cook over medium-high heat until wine evaporates, stirring frequently. Add stock a ladleful at a time. Cook until stock evaporates and risotto is tender but firm, stirring constantly. Layer rice, eggplant slices, tomato mixture and Parmesan cheese $^1/_2$ at a time in 9x13-inch baking dish lightly greased with olive oil. Top with mozzarella cheese. Bake at 350 degrees for 15 minutes.

Serves 10

Tomato, Basil and Cheese Tart

■ ■ ■ ■ ■

1¼ cups flour   ¼ teaspoon salt
6 tablespoons cold unsalted butter, chopped
2 tablespoons cold vegetable shortening
4 ounces crisp-cooked lean bacon, crumbled
3 to 4 tablespoons ice water
4 large (about 2 pounds) firm ripe tomatoes
Salt to taste   1 cup firmly packed fresh basil leaves
½ cup plus 2 tablespoons whole milk ricotta cheese
2 eggs, lightly beaten   1½ teaspoons salt
1 cup coarsely shredded whole milk mozzarella cheese
½ cup freshly grated Parmesan cheese   Pepper to taste
¼ cup (or more) vegetable oil   3 basil sprigs

*M*ix the flour and ¼ teaspoon salt in a bowl. Cut in butter and shortening until crumbly. Add bacon. Add water 1 tablespoonful at a time, mixing with a fork until mixture forms a ball. Knead until blended. Flatten slightly; dust with additional flour. Chill, wrapped in waxed paper, in the refrigerator for 1 hour. Roll dough ⅛ inch thick on a floured surface. Fit into a 9-inch tart pan with a removable fluted rim. Prick lightly with a fork. Chill for 30 minutes. Line shell with foil. Fill with uncooked rice. Bake at 425 degrees for 15 minutes. Remove foil and rice. Bake for 3 minutes longer or until light golden brown. Cool. Slice the tomatoes ⅓ inch thick. Sprinkle with salt; drain on paper towels and pat dry. Purée the basil leaves and ricotta cheese. Add eggs; process until blended. Add 1½ teaspoons salt, cheeses and pepper. Process just until mixed. Layer tomato end pieces and cheese mixture in shell. Arrange overlapping tomato slices on top. Brush with oil. Bake at 350 degrees for 40 minutes or until set. Let stand for 10 minutes. Garnish with basil sprigs.

Serves 6

With permission of *GOURMET* magazine.

Sara Moulton

Joining GOURMET *magazine as food editor in 1984, Sara Moulton became executive chef of* GOURMET's *dining room in 1988. She is co-founder of the New York Woman's Culinary Alliance and helped found the Woman's Culinary Guild of New England. She has worked with Julia Child as associate chef on "More Julia and Company" and as executive chef of Child's segments of "Good Morning America," where she currently serves as back-up chef. Sara graduated with honors from the Culinary Institute of America and was awarded a scholarship from Les Dames D'Escoffier for her achievement.*

Exley/Virginia Slims Legends

Billie Jean King

A professional tennis legend, Billie Jean King was ranked number one in the world five times and number one in the U.S. seven times. The holder of a record 20 Wimbledon titles, she was ranked in the top 10 in the world for 17 years. Billie Jean King is currently the Director and Official Spokesperson of WORLD TEAMTENNIS, which has attracted more than 380,000 participants to its regional leagues and features eight teams in its 1996 professional season. As Director of TEAM-TENNIS, she is the first woman commissioner in professional sports history.

■

A couple of very important pieces of advice for you to recall are: "Be true to yourself. Learn to recognize your own truth and stay focused in life. Always remember to go for it and remind yourself, 'Yes, I am the best!'"

Veggie and Rice Stir-Fry

■ ■ ■ ■ ■

1¹/₂ cups water
1¹/₂ cups uncooked rice
2 tablespoons virgin olive oil
1 cup sliced fresh mushrooms
1 cup bamboo shoots
1 cup broccoli florets
1 cup cauliflower florets
1 cup sliced carrots
1 cup pea pods
1 cup chopped onion
¹/₄ cup (or more) soy sauce

Bring the water to a boil in a saucepan. Add the rice. Cook over medium heat for 5 to 7 minutes or until the rice is done to taste. Remove from the heat. Let stand for 5 minutes. Heat the olive oil in a wok until a drop of water bubbles when dropped in the oil. Add the vegetables. Stir-fry on medium heat for 3 to 4 minutes, adding 1 tablespoon of water if the vegetables appear dry. Add soy sauce. Stir-fry for 1 minute longer or until the soy sauce is absorbed. Drain the vegetables to remove the excess oil. Serve the rice and vegetables in separate serving bowls with additional soy sauce for seasoning. May add Aryu-Veda spices for extra flavoring. The amount of vegetables and rice may be varied according to availability and number of servings required.

Serves 8

Vegetable Terrine

■ ■ ■ ■ ■

1 pound yellow summer squash, coarsely grated

2 teaspoons salt   1 pound red bell peppers, julienned

3 hard-cooked eggs, finely chopped

2¹/₂ cups cooked rice, cooled

3 tablespoons minced dill   1 tablespoon minced parsley

2 tablespoons minced shallots or onion

5 tablespoons butter   2 cups finely julienned carrots

Freshly ground pepper and salt to taste

2 cups finely chopped broccoli, blanched   6 eggs, beaten

1¹/₃ cups cream   ¹/₄ cup dried bread crumbs

1 cup shredded Swiss cheese

Toss squash with 2 teaspoons salt in a bowl. Drain in a sieve for 30 minutes. Mix squash and red peppers in a bowl. Mix chopped eggs, rice, dill and parsley in a bowl. Sauté shallots in ¹/₂ tablespoon butter just until wilted; add to rice mixture. Sauté carrots in 1¹/₂ tablespoons butter for 5 minutes or until soft but not brown; add pepper and salt. Cool. Sauté broccoli in 1¹/₂ tablespoons butter for 5 minutes. Cool. Beat eggs with cream. Line a 5x9-inch loaf pan with buttered waxed paper. Layer half the crumbs, half the rice mixture, ¹/₄ cup cheese, enough egg mixture to cover, carrots, ¹/₄ cup cheese, egg mixture, broccoli, ¹/₄ cup cheese, egg mixture, squash mixture, ¹/₄ cup cheese, egg mixture, remaining rice mixture, egg mixture and remaining crumbs in the prepared pan. Top with buttered waxed paper; cover with foil. Place pan in a deep baking pan; add boiling water to halfway cover sides of loaf pan. Bake at 350 degrees for 1¹/₂ hours or until egg mixture is thickened. Let stand for 10 to 15 minutes. Run a knife around the edges to loosen. Remove foil and top waxed paper. Invert onto a serving plate, removing waxed paper carefully.

Serves 12

Marian Morash

The hostess of the recipe segment of "The Victory Garden," a Public Television gardening series, Marian Morash gives gardeners all the tips they need to know about preparing, cooking, storing, freezing, and preserving vegetables. With gardeners continuing to ask her what they should do with the wonderful vegetables they've grown, she published The Victory Garden Cookbook *in 1982. The book is a vegetable encyclopedia for gardeners who cook and cooks who wish to garden. The mother of two daughters, Morash also served as executive chef on the "Julia Child and More Company" television series.*

Marian Morash, *The Victory Garden Cookbook*, 1982, Alfred A. Knopf Inc.

Michael Quan Photography

Barbara Dawson

When Barbara Dawson's children entered nursery school, she was involved in an automobile accident which caused her instant and total blindness. However, she considered this a challenge, not an obstacle. After her youngest child became a full-time student, she went back to school and earned her master's degree in public relations and a certificate of advanced graduate study in adult education. During this time, she worked through the Massachusetts Society for the Prevention of Blindness to pass federal regulations that required eyeglass lenses to be made of shatterproof or impact-resistant materials.

■

Live by the Bible verse, "To whom much is given, much is expected."

Basic White Bread Recipe

■ ■ ■ ■ ■

1 cake yeast or 1 package dry yeast
¼ cup lukewarm water
1 cup milk, scalded
2 tablespoons sugar
2 teaspoons salt
1¼ cups cold water
6 cups flour, sifted
1 tablespoon melted shortening

*C*rumble the yeast into ¼ cup lukewarm water. Let stand for 5 minutes to soften. Combine the scalded milk, sugar, salt and 1¼ cups cold water in a large bowl, mixing well. Let stand until lukewarm. Add the yeast, stirring until dissolved. Add ½ of the flour, stirring until well mixed. Stir in the shortening. Add the remaining flour, stirring until thoroughly mixed. Knead the dough for 12 minutes. Place the dough in a greased bowl, turning to grease the surface. Let rise in a draft-free warm place (82 to 86 degrees) for 2½ hours or until doubled in bulk. Punch the dough down. Let rise for 1 hour or until doubled in bulk. Shape into 2 loaves and place in 2 greased 5x9-inch loaf pans. Let rise, covered, for 45 to 60 minutes or until doubled in bulk. Bake at 400 degrees for 50 minutes or until the bread tests done. Invert onto a wire rack to cool. May substitute ½ cup evaporated milk and ½ cup water for the milk. May replace ½ of the flour with 3 cups of any combination of flours, such as oatmeal, multigrain oats, wheat or rye.

Serves 24

Meringue Coffee Cake

■ ■ ■ ■ ■

**1/2 cup water
2 cups sugar
Several drops of vanilla extract
5 egg whites
2 teaspoons instant coffee
3 cups milk
5 egg yolks, beaten
2 teaspoons vanilla extract**

*B*ring the water to a boil in a saucepan over medium heat. Stir in the sugar. Cook over medium heat until thickened, stirring frequently. Add several drops of vanilla. Beat the egg whites in a mixer bowl until soft peaks form. Add the instant coffee and sugar syrup gradually, beating until stiff peaks form. Spoon into a buttered tube pan. Bake at 350 degrees for 20 minutes or until set. Invert onto serving plate. Cool before serving. Heat the milk in a saucepan until it reaches the boiling point. Stir a small amount of the milk into the egg yolks in a small bowl. Add the egg yolks to the hot milk, mixing well. Add 2 teaspoons vanilla. Beat for 15 minutes or until the sauce cools. Serve over the Meringue Coffee Cake.

Serves 8

■

As in cooking and as in living, tenderly mix the ingredients at your own pace. Be daring in your intuition when adding special flavors. Be patient while you stir, and most of all, be grateful for the joys of the earth, the hands that cooked this, and the spirit of sharing the wisdom of the palate.

T. Polumbaum

Marjorie Agosin

Professor of Spanish at Wellesley College in Massachusetts, Marjorie Agosin is a literary critic, humanitarian and an acclaimed poet. Author of noted books such as Toward the Splendid City, Circles of Madness: Mothers of the Plaza de Mayo, A Cross and a Star, *and* Noche Estrellada, *she was awarded the 1995 Latino Literature Prize for poetry by the Latin-American Writers Institute, and the Letras de Oro Prize for poetry presented by Spain's Ministry of Culture and the North-South Center of the University of Miami. These are the two highest honors presented for works by Latin-American writers.*

■

Lidia Bastianich

Widely regarded as the "First Lady" of Italian restaurants in the United States, Lidia Bastianich has left an indelible mark on New York City as a food historian, executive chef and co-owner of three restaurants. Through her restaurants (Felidia, Becco, and Frico Bar), lectures, a cookbook, and frequent yearly travels to Italy, she is credited with having helped bring "authentic" Italian cooking to the American public. Since 1994, Lidia has also been running a food catalog entitled Il Cibo Di Lidia. In her book, La Cucina Di Lidia, she has assembled a collection of 120 simple, but sophisticated family recipes that are spiced with tidbits of history and traditions of her homeland in Pula, Istria, a region formed by the Gulf of Trieste at the juncture of Italy and the former Yugoslavia.

Educate and prepare yourself properly, then affront your career as a professional, not as a woman.

Gnocchi Fritti

■ ■ ■ ■ ■

1 cake yeast
1 cup warm milk
1 tablespoon olive oil
2$\frac{1}{2}$ pounds flour
1 teaspoon salt
1$\frac{1}{2}$ cups mineral water
3 cups vegetable oil
Salt to taste
Slices of Prosciutto di Parma

*S*often the yeast in the warm milk. Combine the yeast, milk and olive oil in a mixer bowl. Mix well with a mixer fitted with dough hooks. Add the flour, mixing at slow speed. Add 1 teaspoon salt and mineral water. Mix at slow speed for 20 minutes. Wrap the dough in a damp towel. Let rest for 15 minutes at room temperature. Divide the dough into 5 portions. Roll each portion $\frac{1}{4}$ inch thick. Cut into rounds or squares with a 2-inch diameter cookie cutter. Fry a few at a time in hot vegetable oil in a large saucepan until golden brown. Drain on paper towels. Salt lightly and serve warm with thin slices of Prosciutto di Parma.

Serves 6

Jalapeño Cheese Corn Bread

■ ■ ■ ■ ■

This wonderful recipe is particularly good with chicken, pork or any vegetable.

1½ cups corn bread mix   ¾ cup milk
1 egg   ½ green onion, chopped
½ cup cream-style corn
¼ cup chopped jalapeño pepper
¾ cup shredded Cheddar cheese or
Monterey Jack cheese   1 tablespoon sugar
2 tablespoons vegetable oil
¼ cup bacon bits, or to taste
¼ cup pimento, or to taste
Minced garlic to taste

Combine the corn bread mix, milk, egg, green onion, corn, jalapeño pepper, cheese, sugar, oil, bacon bits, pimento and garlic in a bowl and mix well. Pour into a buttered 9x13-inch baking dish. Bake at 425 degrees for 25 minutes or until brown.

Serves 8

■

My advice to you: 1) Read awhile before going to sleep each night. 2) Do not be afraid of failure. You often learn more from the errors in life than from your successes. 3) Do keep your mind open for new ideas. 4) Do respect others, regardless of their ability, race, religion, or gender. Be accepting of diversity. 5) Don't do physical harm to yourself or others. 6) Don't be in a hurry to be an adult. It lasts a long time. 7) Don't cause a pregnancy or become pregnant until you can financially support a child. 8) And most important, gain as much education as possible.

Ann Richards

Ann Richards has come a long way from her first involvement in politics as a graduate student at the University of Texas at Austin. It was there she started fighting for civil rights and economic justice—interests that led to her position as Governor of Texas. Along the way, she raised four children, taught junior high school, and was elected to be a county commissioner and then state treasurer for the Lone Star State. As the state's 45th Governor, she worked hard to ensure that her four grandchildren lived in "a Texas where people come first."

Sally Jessy Raphaël

The first woman talk show host, Sally Jessy Raphaël has managed to keep her show the second-highest-rated topical talk show amidst ever-growing controversy and competition. The only talk show host who is the mother of grown children, she is currently seen in almost 180 markets nationwide. Her show received an Emmy Award for Outstanding Talk Show in 1990 and for Outstanding Talk Show Host in 1989 from the National Academy of Television Arts & Sciences.

■

Don't take _ _ _ _ from anyone! Never depend on anyone else. Be self-sufficient. It's O.K. to love a man but not to live for a man.

Nutty Nutmeg Muffins

■ ■ ■ ■ ■

2 cups flour
3 tablespoons sugar
1 tablespoon baking powder
¹/₂ teaspoon freshly grated nutmeg, or
1 teaspoon ground
¹/₄ teaspoon salt
¹/₂ cup chopped walnuts
2 eggs
1 cup milk
¹/₄ cup melted butter

*C*ombine the flour, sugar, baking powder, nutmeg and salt in a bowl and mix well. Stir in the walnuts. Combine the eggs, milk and butter in a bowl and whisk together. Fold into the dry ingredients just until mixed. Grease 12 regular or 36 miniature muffin cups or line with paper baking cups. Fill each muffin cup ²/₃ full. Bake at 375 degrees for 15 to 20 minutes or until light brown. Cool on a wire rack. Serve with apple butter or preserves.

Serves 12

Low-Fat Oat Bran Muffins

■ ■ ■ ■ ■

1 cup oat bran
1 cup whole wheat flour
1 tablespoon baking powder
³/₄ teaspoon nutmeg
1 teaspoon cinnamon
¹/₄ cup canola oil
³/₄ cup unsweetened apple juice concentrate
2 egg whites, stiffly beaten
1 cup fresh or frozen blueberries

*C*ombine the oat bran, whole wheat flour, baking powder, nutmeg and cinnamon in a bowl and mix well. Combine the canola oil and apple juice concentrate in a bowl. Add to the dry ingredients and mix well. Fold in the egg whites and blueberries gently. Spoon into 6 greased muffin cups. Bake at 400 degrees for 20 to 25 minutes or until the muffins test done. Remove to a wire rack to cool.

Serves 6

■

This world into which you were born is far from the best of all possible worlds. And we must apologize for that. And even though there are people who have done their share of speaking out...and sitting in...and standing up...it's still a long way from a just and peaceful world. Someday it will be your turn.

Marilyn Bergman

The recipient of three Academy Awards, three Emmy Awards, two Grammy Awards, and an Ace Award, Marilyn Bergman is one-half of the most respected song-writing team today. With her husband, Alan, Marilyn Bergman won the Academy Award in 1968, 1973, and 1984 for the songs "The Windmills of Your Mind," "The Way We Were," and for the score of Yentl. Since their first Oscar nomination in 1968, they have been nominated 16 times. This year, they were nominated for both a Golden Globe and an Academy Award for their song "Moonlight," recorded by Sting for the Sydney Pollack film Sabrina. In February, 1994, after being the first woman elected to the Board of Directors of the American Society of Composers and Producers and serving five terms, Marilyn Bergman was elected President and Chairman of the Board.

Irene Young

Washington Sisters

The Washington Sisters, Sharon and Sändra, have brought an uplifting spirit of hope to concert and festival audiences across the U.S. and Canada since 1984. Their blend of a cappella, jazz swing, blues, gospel and island rhythms provides a unique basis for their message of peace, women's rights, and cultural diversity. They have two recordings, Take Two *and* Understated.

Sharon J. Washington, Ph.D., is the president of TapestryWorks, *which conducts educational workshops and consultations on diversity, adventure education and organizational development. She is an associate professor at Springfield College in the education department, and serves on the board of directors of a local arts organization.*

Sändra J. Washington works as a planner with the National Park Service to encourage community-based conservation projects, and is excited by the opportunity to explore the ways conservation, recreation, historic preservation and art can be tapped for revitalization of urban neighborhoods.

Washington Family Waffles

■ ■ ■ ■ ■

2 cups flour
3 teaspoons baking powder
1/4 teaspoon baking soda
1/8 teaspoon salt   4 egg yolks
2 cups buttermilk
1 cup melted butter, slightly cooled
4 egg whites, stiffly beaten

*C*ombine the flour, baking powder, baking soda and salt in a bowl and mix well. Add the egg yolks and buttermilk; mix well. Stir in the butter. Fold in the egg whites. Bake in a hot nonstick or oiled 10-inch waffle iron using manufacturer's directions for 4 minutes or until the steam has slowed. May substitute 1 percent buttermilk and use only half the amount of butter to lower the fat content. If you substitute margarine, please do not credit us with the results.

Serves 9

■

Sharon: Acknowledge that you stand on the shoulders of those who came before, live today with an awareness of your potential and connection to all people, and know that your life in the present is the legacy of those in the future.

Sändra: It is important to be honest with others and crucial to be true to yourself, your values, your beliefs. What will set you apart in the world is your capacity to show compassion toward others.

Celebrating Success

Women's accomplishments sing out the
quiet elegance of the sweet taste of success.

Donna Paul

Lora A. Brody

Lora Brody has taken her place among America's most respected culinary personalities as an author, spokesperson, lecturer, cooking instructor and multimedia personality. For nearly two decades she has been an influential force in American food trends, as well as a guide and mentor for the home cook. A best-selling cookbook author, Lora Brody has published 14 books of her own and appeared in numerous others. She has also done consulting with major corporations in the food industry, helped found The Women's Culinary Guild, and has appeared on countless television and radio programs.

Bête Noire

■ ■ ■ ■ ■

12 ounces best-quality white chocolate, broken
$^{1}/_{2}$ cup whipping cream
$^{2}/_{3}$ cup Truffles white chocolate liqueur
$1^{1}/_{3}$ cups superfine sugar $^{1}/_{2}$ cup water
8 ounces unsweetened chocolate, broken
4 ounces bittersweet chocolate, broken
1 cup unsalted butter, softened, cut into chunks
5 extra-large eggs, at room temperature

*P*lace the white chocolate pieces in a blender container. Mix the cream and white chocolate liqueur in a small saucepan. Heat gently to just below the boiling point. Pour over the white chocolate. Process until smooth. Chill for 24 hours before using. Combine 1 cup of the sugar and the water in a medium saucepan. Cook over medium heat until the sugar is dissolved and the mixture begins to boil. Remove from the heat. Add the unsweetened and bittersweet chocolate, stirring until dissolved. Add the butter 1 chunk at a time, stirring until melted after each addition. Beat the eggs with the remaining sugar in a bowl until foamy and slightly thickened. Add to the chocolate mixture, whisking well. Grease a 9-inch cake pan. Line the bottom with parchment paper; grease. Pour the batter into the prepared pan. Place the cake pan inside a larger pan filled with 1 inch of hot water. Place on the center rack in the oven. Bake at 350 degrees for 30 minutes. Top will be crusty but cake will be moist. Remove from the oven. Cover the cake with plastic wrap and invert onto a baking sheet. Remove the parchment paper. Cover with a flat plate and invert again. Serve hot or at room temperature, topped with the white chocolate creme.

Serves 12

Lora Brody, *Growing up on the Chocolate Diet*, Little, Brown and Company, 1983.

Sour Cherry Blintzes

■ ■ ■ ■ ■

12 ounces mascarpone cheese
1 tablespoon sugar
$^3/_4$ teaspoon vanilla extract
$^1/_8$ teaspoon salt   12 crêpes
$4^1/_2$ cups pitted sour cherries
$2^1/_2$ cups water $^1/_4$ cup Grand Marnier
1 tablespoon sugar
$^1/_2$ cup orange juice
$2^1/_2$ teaspoons cornstarch
3 tablespoons clarified unsalted butter

*C*ombine the cheese, 1 tablespoon sugar, vanilla and salt in a small bowl; mix well. Place 2 teaspoons of the mixture onto each crêpe, spreading to within 1 inch of the edge. Roll up, tucking in the ends and securing with a pinch of the cheese. Combine the sour cherries and the water in a saucepan. Cook over medium heat for 15 minutes or until the cherries are plumped. Remove the cherries with a slotted spoon, reserving the juice. Stir the Grand Marnier, 1 tablespoon sugar, orange juice and cornstarch into the juice in the saucepan. Cook over medium heat for 5 to 10 minutes or until thickened. Return the cherries to the sauce. Remove from heat and cover to keep warm. Heat the clarified butter in a sauté pan. Place the crêpes seam side down in the sauté pan. Cook for 1 to 2 minutes or until browned; turn and brown the other side. Place 2 crêpes on each serving plate. Spoon the cherries and sauce over the crêpes. Serve immediately.

Serves 6

Emily Luchetti

A pastry chef and cookbook author, former Girl Scout Emily Luchetti is the president of the International Association of Women Chefs and Restaurateurs. A pastry chef at Stars Restaurant in San Francisco from 1987 to 1995, she was nominated by the James Beard Society in 1994 and 1995 as the Best Pastry Chef in the United States. Emily's new book, entitled Four-Star Desserts, *is due out in the fall of 1996.*

■

Do not underestimate your abilities. You will be amazed at what you can accomplish when you put your heart and mind into a project. If you fail at something, do not get too discouraged. We learn from our mistakes as much as from our successes. Remember <u>everyone</u> makes mistakes, even famous and successful people and people you think "have it all together." No one goes through life without making mistakes.

Johanne Killeen

Along with her husband, Johanne Killeen is both chef and owner of Al Forno Restaurant in Providence, Rhode Island, recently hailed as the "Best Casual Restaurant in the World" by the International Herald Tribune. *Their cooking has been featured in every major food magazine in the U.S. The team has earned numerous awards, including the James Beard Award for the Best Chefs in the Northeast, the Golden Dish Award from* Gentleman's Quarterly *for "Johanne's Lemon Meringue Tart" recipe, and the prestigious Distinguished Restaurants of North America Award. The co-authors of a successful cookbook, they also received the Ivy Award in May from their peers in the international cooking industry.*

Tartufo Ice Cream

■ ■ ■ ■ ■

No truffles in this ice cream. Just rich, dense, delicious chocolate and unsweetened whipped cream.

$2^1/_2$ cups milk
4 egg yolks
$^1/_2$ cup sugar
8 ounces unsweetened chocolate, chopped
8 ounces semisweetened chocolate, chopped
5 tablespoons whipping cream

Scald the milk in a heavy saucepan. Whisk the egg yolks and sugar in a large bowl. Add the hot milk gradually, whisking constantly. Return the mixture to the saucepan. Cook over low heat for 5 to 10 minutes or until the custard coats the back of a spoon, stirring constantly. Combine the unsweetened and half the semisweetened chocolate in a bowl over simmering water. Heat until melted, stirring frequently. Strain the custard through a fine mesh strainer into the melted chocolate, whisking constantly. Whisk in the cream. Chill well. Pour into an ice cream freezer. Freeze according to the manufacturer's instructions. Add the remaining semisweet chocolate pieces about 5 minutes before the ice cream is ready. Serve with unsweetened whipped cream.

Serves 10

Chocolate Bread Pudding

■ ■ ■ ■ ■

4 cups French sourdough bread cubes
3¹/₂ cups half-and-half   2 teaspoons vanilla extract
1 tablespoon Kahlúa   ¹/₈ teaspoon salt
2 ounces unsweetened chocolate   ¹/₂ cup strong coffee
1 tablespoon butter   3 egg yolks
1 cup sugar   ¹/₄ to 1 teaspoon lemon zest
¹/₈ teaspoon cinnamon   ³/₄ cup whipping cream
1 tablespoon sugar   1 tablespoon unsalted butter
4 ounces semisweet chocolate, shredded
2 tablespoons Kahlúa
¹/₂ cup coarsely chopped black or English walnuts
1 cup whipping cream, whipped   1 teaspoon vanilla extract

Soak the bread cubes in a mixture of the next 4 ingredients at room temperature for 2 hours. Melt 2 ounces chocolate, coffee and 1 tablespoon butter in a saucepan over low heat. Stir into the bread cube mixture. Beat the egg yolks in a mixer bowl until light and frothy. Beat in 1 cup sugar gradually. Strain 2 cups of the cream mixture from the bread cubes. Add to the egg mixture, beating until blended. Stir the bread mixture into the egg mixture. Add the lemon zest and cinnamon. Spoon into a greased 9x13-inch baking pan; cover with foil. Place in a larger pan. Add enough water to reach ²/₃ up the sides of the smaller pan. Bake at 350 degrees for 40 minutes or until set. Let stand for 15 minutes or longer. Bring ³/₄ cup whipping cream, 1 table-spoon sugar and 1 tablespoon butter to a simmer in a saucepan. Remove from heat. Stir in 4 ounces chocolate, 2 tablespoons Kahlúa and walnuts. Blend whipped cream with 1 teaspoon vanilla. Spoon into a pastry bag fitted with star tip. Spoon bread pudding into dessert dishes; drizzle with the sauce. Pipe the whipped cream over the top. Garnish with chocolate shavings.

Serves 8

Anne Herman

Jimella Lucas and Nanci Main

Authors of The Ark: Cuisine of the Pacific Northwest, *Nanci Main and Jimella Lucas are award-winning owner/chefs of The Ark Restaurant. Listed among* Food and Wine's *Outstanding Young Chefs of America, the two trained and worked in restaurants throughout the Northwest before joining up to open the Shelburne Restaurant in Seaview, Washington, in 1980. Their national acclaim has grown consistently since food critic James Beard wrote his first column about them in 1981. Publishing their second set of recipes from their restaurant in a book entitled* Bay and Ocean: Ark Restaurant Cuisine, *they have also been featured in such magazines as* Newsweek, Town and Country, *and* Chocolatier.

■

Work hard, don't whine,
don't compromise on what you value
and believe, do forgive yourself
and others daily.

Ken Regan/HBO

Dr. Jane Goodall

The author of six major books, countless articles, and the recipient of numerous prestigious awards, Dr. Jane Goodall remains one of the most renowned and respected scientists in the world. After more than 35 years of research, Dr. Jane Goodall is still contributing significant findings on chimpanzee behavior. Her scientific discoveries have laid the foundation for all primate studies and have transformed natural history field studies. In 1960, Dr. Jane Goodall arrived on the shores of Lake Tanganyika in Tanzania, East Africa. There, she met famed anthropologist and paleontologist Dr. Louis Leakey. Soon afterwards, Dr. Leakey chose Jane to pioneer a pivotal field study of chimpanzees. She later established the Gombe Stream Research Center and astonished the world with such studies as her observations of chimps making and using tools—a behavior previously believed to separate man from other animals. In 1977, she founded The Jane Goodall Institute for Wildlife Research, Education and Conservation.

Crème Brûlée

■ ■ ■ ■ ■

Whipping cream is used in the classic recipe, but it is acceptable to substitute half the whipping cream with evaporated milk.

2 cups whipping cream
4 eggs or 8 egg yolks
³/₄ cup packed brown sugar
¹/₄ teaspoon salt
¹/₄ to ¹/₂ cup packed light brown sugar

*S*cald the whipping cream in a double boiler over hot water. Remove from heat. Beat the eggs, ³/₄ cup brown sugar and salt in a mixer bowl until smooth. Stir a small amount of the hot whipping cream into the egg mixture; stir the egg mixture into the whipping cream. Cook over low heat for 7 minutes or just until thickened, beating constantly with an electric or hand beater. Pour into a shallow ovenproof dish to a depth of 2 inches. Let stand until cool. Chill, covered, for 2 to 8 hours or until the top is set. Sift ¹/₄ to ¹/₂ cup brown sugar over the top. Place in a cold oven. Broil until brown, rotating the dish to allow even browning. Watch carefully to prevent sugar from burning. Chill for 4 hours or until the glaze is firm and crackly.

Serves 6

■

Follow your dreams. Every individual matters; every individual makes a difference.

Fanny Farmer Cookbook.

Pavlova

■ ■ ■ ■ ■

Meringue Shell
1¹/₂ cups whipping cream
3 tablespoons sugar
¹/₂ teaspoon vanilla extract   2 cups strawberry halves
1 (8-ounce) can pineapple tidbits, drained
1 star fruit, sliced
1 kiwifruit, cut into halves lengthwise, sliced

*A*rrange the Meringue Shell on a serving platter. Beat the whipping cream in a mixer bowl until soft peaks form. Add the sugar and vanilla and mix well. Spread the shell with the whipped cream. Decorate with the fruit.

Meringue Shell

4 egg whites   1 cup sugar
¹/₄ cup cornstarch   1¹/₂ teaspoons white vinegar
¹/₂ teaspoon vanilla extract

*G*rease a baking sheet; line with waxed paper and grease the waxed paper. Draw an 8-inch circle on the waxed paper. Beat the egg whites in a mixer bowl until soft peaks form. Add the sugar gradually, beating constantly until stiff peaks form. Beat in the cornstarch, vinegar and vanilla until blended. Spread the meringue with a rubber spatula over the circle on the prepared baking sheet, building up the sides to form a 2-inch rim. Bake at 225 degrees for 2 hours or until the surface is dry but not brown. Turn off the oven. Let stand in the oven with the door slightly ajar until cool.

Serves 12

Linda Fuller

Co-founder of Habitat for Humanity International, with her husband, Linda Fuller launched the ecumenical Christian housing ministry in 1976 after pioneering low-cost housing programs in rural southwest Georgia and in the African country of Zaire. The Fullers initiated several partnership enterprises at Koinonia Farm, a Christian community, including a ministry in housing based on several unique features that they developed including no-profit, no-interest mortgages and the requirement that homeowners contribute "sweat equity" into their future homes.

■

Money, power and high position may look appealing at a distance, but they come with a great price tag. I think each person has to decide what is important and what has real value in life.

Michael Provost

Tania León

In demand as both composer and conductor, and one of the most vital personalities on today's music scene, Tania León has also been recognized for her significant accomplishments as educator and as advisor to arts organizations. Tania León was appointed Revson Composer Fellow by the New York Philharmonic in January, 1993, a three-year post in which she advised Music Director Kurt Masur on contemporary music. As of 1996, she has been named the New Music Advisor of the Philharmonic. She is also the Artistic Director of the American Composers Orchestra's annual festival Sonidos de las Americas, and is advisor of Meet the Composer's New Residencies Program. León's first opera, Scourge of Hyacinths, won the BMW prize for Best Composition of the 1994 Münchener Biennale for New Music Theatre. Tania León is professor of music at Brooklyn College, where she has taught since 1985, and has served as a visiting lecturer at Harvard and Yale Universities.

Stuffed Chayote

■ ■ ■ ■ ■

2 chayotes, cut into halves
Salt to taste
³/₄ cup milk
2 teaspoons flour
¹/₄ cup sugar
2 egg yolks
1 cinnamon stick
¹/₂ cup raisins
1 teaspoon vanilla extract
¹/₂ cup sliced almonds
Ground cinnamon to taste

*C*ombine the chayotes and salt with enough water to cover in a saucepan. Boil until tender; drain. Cool slightly. Remove the chayote pulp carefully, leaving the shells intact. Press the pulp through a colander into a saucepan. Combine the milk and flour in a bowl, stirring until blended. Add the sugar, egg yolks and cinnamon stick and mix well. Add to the pulp and mix well. Cook over low heat until thickened, stirring constantly. Remove from heat. Stir in the raisins and vanilla. Discard the cinnamon stick. Spoon into the chayote shells. Sprinkle with the almonds and ground cinnamon. Chill until serving time. May serve any remaining pulp mixture in individual dishes.

Serves 4

■

Believe in yourself and pursue your dreams.

Red White and Blue Cobbler

■ ■ ■ ■ ■

¹/₄ **cup sugar**

1¹/₂ **teaspoons cornstarch**

2 cups fresh or frozen unsweetened blueberries

¹/₂ **teaspoon lemon juice**

1 (21-ounce) can cherry pie filling

¹/₂ **cup plus 2 tablespoons sugar**

1¹/₂ **tablespoons cornstarch**

¹/₈ **teaspoon cinnamon**

¹/₈ **teaspoon almond extract**

1 cup flour   1 tablespoon sugar

1¹/₂ **teaspoons baking powder**

¹/₂ **teaspoon salt**

3 tablespoons shortening   ¹/₂ cup milk

Barbara Bush

Former First Lady of the United States, Barbara Bush has dedicated her life to charity and humanitarian causes. With family literacy as her number one cause, she founded the Barbara Bush Foundation for Family Literacy and currently serves as the Foundation's Honorary Chair. She believes that if more people could read, write and comprehend, we would be that much closer to solving so many of the problems plaguing our society today.

*C*ombine ¹/₄ cup sugar and 1¹/₂ teaspoons cornstarch in a saucepan and mix well. Stir in the blueberries and lemon juice. Cook until thickened, stirring frequently. Spoon into an 8x8-inch baking dish. Place in a 250-degree oven to keep warm. Drain the cherries, reserving the juice and cherries. Combine ¹/₂ cup plus 2 tablespoons sugar, 1¹/₂ tablespoons cornstarch and cinnamon in a saucepan and mix well. Add the reserved cherry juice gradually and mix well. Cook until thickened, stirring frequently. Add the cherries and flavoring and mix gently. Spread over the prepared layer. Keep warm in the oven. Combine the flour, 1 tablespoon sugar, baking powder and salt in a bowl and mix well. Cut in the shortening until crumbly. Stir in the milk. Drop by spoonfuls over the prepared layers. Bake at 400 degrees for 25 to 30 minutes or until brown.

Serves 6

■

Each of us has gifts and talents our communities need. I find that sharing myself with others brings me great comfort. Perhaps similar efforts will bring you strength and courage. The friends you make in the Girl Scouts, the kind deeds you do for others, the love of your family and faith in God will lead you towards a happy full life.

James Kegley

Ann Amernick

Ann Amernick, one of the most highly regarded pastry chefs and authors in the United States, creates private specialty pastries in Washington, D.C. She has been a pastry chef at many noted restaurants in the area and was the assistant pastry chef at the White House in 1980 and 1981. Ann is the author of two cookbooks, including Special Desserts, *and was a nominee for Pastry Chef of the Year by the James Beard Foundation. The winner of many awards and recognitions, she was named one of the Ten Best Pastry Chefs in America by* Chocolatier *Magazine in 1994, and was recognized in* Who's Who of American Women, *17th Edition.*

■

Follow your dreams. Don't give up—think of others.

Peanut Butter Truffles

■ ■ ■ ■ ■

1^1/$_4$ cups whipping cream
1 pound milk chocolate, chopped
^{1}/$_2$ cup unsalted butter, softened
^{1}/$_2$ cup packed dark brown sugar
1 cup confectioners' sugar
1 cup plain pure peanut butter
1 cup chunky pure peanut butter
2 cups whipping cream
8 ounces bittersweet chocolate, chopped

*B*ring 1^1/$_4$ cups whipping cream to a boil in a saucepan. Remove from heat. Add the milk chocolate, stirring until blended. Chill for 30 minutes or until lukewarm. Combine the butter, brown sugar, confectioners' sugar and peanut butter in a mixer bowl. Beat at medium speed for 2 minutes or until blended. Shape into balls ^{1}/$_2$ inch in diameter. May chill the mixture for 45 minutes or longer before shaping. Place 1 peanut ball at a time on a parchment-lined tray; press with thumb to ^{1}/$_4$ inch thick. Repeat the procedure with the remaining mixture. Beat the milk chocolate mixture in a mixer bowl with the whisk attachment until light in color and fluffy. Spoon into a pastry bag fitted with a ^{1}/$_4$-inch plain tip. Pipe a mound on top of each truffle, swirling to finish the pipe. Chill for 1 hour or until firm; cover with plastic wrap. Chill until serving time. Bring 2 cups whipping cream to a boil in a saucepan. Remove from heat. Stir in the bittersweet chocolate until smooth. Spoon about 1^1/$_2$ teaspoons of the chocolate glaze over each truffle, coating as much of the surface as possible.

Serves 24

The Ultimate Brownie

■ ■ ■ ■ ■

**8 ounces semisweet chocolate, chopped
(Lindt Excellence)
14 tablespoons unsalted butter
2 eggs
³/₄ cup sugar
1 teaspoon vanilla extract
¹/₄ cup flour
4 ounces unsalted macadamia nuts, coarsely chopped
Confectioners' sugar to taste**

*C*ombine the chocolate and butter in a double boiler over hot water. Cook over low heat until smooth, stirring frequently. Remove from heat. Beat the eggs in a mixer bowl at high speed for 1 minute. Add the sugar gradually, beating constantly for 4 to 5 minutes or until the mixture is pale yellow and of the consistency of soft-peaked whipped cream. Add the chocolate mixture and vanilla, beating until blended. Sift in the flour and mix well. Fold in the macadamia nuts. Spoon into a greased 8x8-inch baking pan. Bake at 375 degrees for 30 minutes or until the brownies test done. Cool in the pan on a wire rack. Cut into squares. Sprinkle with confectioners' sugar. For an extra-chewy texture, allow the brownies to stand, covered, at room temperature for 8 to 10 hours.

Serves 16

"The Perfect Chocolate Dessert," *Consumers Guide.*

Jim Gipe

Ruth J. Simmons

Having been a member of the faculties of the University of New Orleans, California State University Northridge, Spelman College, and Princeton University, Ruth J. Simmons assumed the presidency of Smith College in July, 1995. Receiving her Ph.D. in Romance Languages and Literatures from Harvard University in 1973, Simmons has been the recipient of a number of prizes and fellowships, including the German DAAD and a Fulbright Fellowship to France.

■

One of the most important goals every person should have is to strive for the highest level of education possible. I particularly encourage girls and women to take advantage of the opportunities girls' schools and women's colleges provide. These institutions can provide an extra measure of challenge in a safe environment in which to grow and gain confidence.

Rear Admiral Marsha Evans

The first woman Surface Assignments Officer in the Bureau of Naval Personnel in 1973, now Rear Admiral Marsha Johnson Evans concurrently served as Senior Navy Social Aide to the President of the United States. She has served as the Middle East Policy Officer on the Staff of the Commander-in-Chief, U.S. Naval Forces Europe; Executive Officer, Recruit Training Command, San Diego; Commanding Officer, Naval Technical Training Center, San Francisco; and a Battalion Officer at the U.S. Naval Academy where she chaired a Women Midshipmen Study Group and served on the Navy's 1987 Women's Study. From June 1993 to July 1995 she was Commander of the Navy Recruiting Command. She currently serves as Superintendent, Naval Postgraduate School, Monterey, California. Rear Admiral Evans was a Girl Scout through high school, to which experience she attributes "opportunities to learn about teamwork, and leadership… and a superb foundation for my career in the naval service."

Lemon Squares

■ ■ ■ ■ ■

1 cup flour
$1/4$ cup confectioners' sugar
$1/2$ cup butter, softened
2 eggs
$3/4$ cup sugar
3 tablespoons fresh lemon juice
2 tablespoons flour
$1/2$ teaspoon baking powder
Confectioners' sugar to taste

*C*ombine 1 cup flour and $1/4$ cup confectioners' sugar in a bowl and mix well. Cut in the butter until crumbly. Pat into an 8x8-inch baking pan. Bake at 350 degrees for 10 to 12 minutes or until brown. Beat the eggs in a mixer bowl until frothy. Add the sugar and lemon juice. Beat for 10 minutes or until thick and smooth, scraping the bowl occasionally. Add a mixture of 2 tablespoons flour and baking powder, mixing just until moistened. Spoon over the baked layer. Bake for 20 to 25 minutes longer or until set. Cool for 10 minutes. Sift confectioners' sugar over the top. Let stand until cool. Cut into thirty-six $1 1/2$-inch squares.

Serves 36

■

Always try to do your best, no matter what the task; study math and sciences so you will have more opportunities and options; and be a good friend—one who treats others as you would like to be treated.

Alfajores de Maicena

■ ■ ■ ■ ■

Enjoy this Argentinean delight!

3¹/₂ tablespoons (50 grams) butter
4 tablespoons (50 grams) sugar
2 eggs
1 teaspoon vanilla extract
1¹/₂ cups (200 grams) cornstarch
6 tablespoons (50 grams) flour
¹/₂ teaspoon baking powder
1 (14-ounce) can sweetened condensed milk
Coconut powder to taste
Melted chocolate (optional)

*B*eat the butter and sugar in a mixer bowl until creamy. Add the eggs 1 at a time, beating well after each addition. Beat in the vanilla. Add a mixture of the cornstarch, flour and baking powder gradually and mix well. Blend in additional flour if dough is sticky. Chill for 1 hour. Pour the condensed milk into a pie plate. Cover with foil and place in a hot water bath. Bake at 425 degrees for 1 hour or until thick and caramel colored. This is known as "dulce de leche." Roll the dough 1 centimeter thick on a lightly floured surface; cut circles 4 to 6 centimeters in diameter. Arrange on an oiled cookie sheet. Bake at 375 degrees for 10 to 15 minutes or until brown. Remove to a wire rack to cool. Build the cookie sandwich or "alfajor" by spreading an abundant amount of the "dulce de leche" on 1 side of half the cookies; top with the remaining cookies. Roll in the coconut powder. Dip half the cookie in the melted chocolate. Chill for 30 minutes before serving.

Makes 12 cookies

Adriana C. Ocampo

Having moved to the U.S. from Argentina, planetary geologist Adriana C. Ocampo began working for the Jet Propulsion Laboratory at the California Institute of Technology while she was still in high school. She has worked on the Viking mission to Mars and is currently working in Flight Projects Mission Operations as the science coordinator to the Near Infrared Mapping Spectrometer (NIMS), an instrument that is part of the Galileo mission to Jupiter. Adriana C. Ocampo has been a major force in promoting scientific and educational cooperation in Space Science between developing and developed countries.

■

I would like to share this mnemonic (STARS) with you:
Smile—life is a great adventure
Transcend to triumph over the negative
Aspire to be the best
Resolve to be true to your heart
Success comes to those that never give up on their dreams.

Kurt Stier

Martha Stewart

America's premier lifestyle authority, Martha Stewart is a household name throughout America. Through her 16 books, Martha Stewart Living magazine, Emmy-award-winning television series, six instructional videos, and frequent lectures, she has displayed her artistic eye and enormous creativity in the area of domestic arts. From refinishing furniture to building a garden trellis to making angel food cake from scratch, Martha Stewart's popularity has earned her a number one spot on ADWEEK's "Ten Hottest Magazines of 1995" list, as well as the title of "Publishing Executive of the Year."

Alexis' Brown Sugar Chocolate Chip Cookies

■ ■ ■ ■ ■

2 cups unsalted butter
3 cups packed brown sugar
1 cup sugar
4 eggs
2 teaspoons vanilla extract
3^1/$_2$ cups flour
1^1/$_2$ teaspoons salt
2 teaspoons baking soda
1^1/$_2$ cups chocolate chips

Beat the butter in a mixer bowl until smooth; add brown sugar and sugar. Beat in the eggs and vanilla. Sift together the flour, salt and baking soda and beat into the mixture. Add chocolate chips. Drop 2 or 3 tablespoonsful of batter 2 inches apart onto a greased baking sheet. Bake at 375 degrees for 8 minutes. Remove from the baking sheet and cool on wire racks. If cookies become hard while still on the baking sheet, place the baking sheet back in the oven for a few seconds to soften them for easy removal.

Makes 30 cookies

Blue Ribbon Chocolate Chip Cookies

■ ■ ■ ■ ■

2¹/₂ cups flour
¹/₂ teaspoon baking soda
¹/₄ teaspoon salt
1 cup packed dark brown sugar
¹/₂ cup sugar
1 cup butter, softened
2 eggs
2 teaspoons vanilla extract
2 cups semisweet chocolate chips

*C*ombine the flour, baking soda and salt in a bowl, mixing with a wire whisk. Combine the brown sugar and sugar in a mixer bowl. Beat at medium speed until blended. Add the butter, beating until of a pasty consistency and scraping the bowl occasionally. Add the eggs and vanilla. Beat at medium speed until light and fluffy. Add the flour mixture. Beat at low speed just until mixed. Fold in the chocolate chips. Drop by rounded tablespoons 2 inches apart onto an ungreased cooked sheet. Bake at 300 degrees for 22 to 24 minutes or until golden brown. Remove to a wire rack to cool.

Makes 42 cookies

Debbi Fields

A wife and mother of five daughters, Debbi Fields supervises operations, brand name management, public relations, and product development of her company, Mrs. Fields Cookies. She began her career at the age of 20 when, without any business experience, she managed to convince a bank to finance her business concept. Today, Mrs. Fields has over 600 company-owned and franchise stores across the United States and in six foreign countries.

■

Never give up. Good enough never is. Always believe in yourself.

Hillary Rodham Clinton

Prior to becoming the First Lady of the United States, Hillary Rodham Clinton worked as a full-time partner of a law firm and chaired the Arkansas Education Standards Committee. She also founded the Arkansas Advocates for Children and Families. Mrs. Clinton also serves as the Honorary President of the Girl Scouts of the U.S.A. A Girl Scout herself, the First Lady has dedicated herself to family, work and community service. In Washington, the First Lady served as chairperson of the Task Force on National Health Care Reform, dedicating 19 months to traveling across the country talking to doctors, nurses, health care professionals and people from all walks of life about ways to improve the health care system and ensure that every American has the right to quality, affordable health care. She has demonstrated her advocacy for children's rights in her recent book, It Takes A Village.

Hillary Clinton's Chocolate Chip Cookies

■ ■ ■ ■ ■

1^1/$_2$ cups flour
1 teaspoon salt
1 teaspoon baking soda
1 cup vegetable shortening
1 cup packed light brown sugar
^{1}/$_2$ cup sugar
1 teaspoon vanilla extract
2 eggs
2 cups old-fashioned rolled oats
2 cups semisweet chocolate chips

*M*ix the flour, salt and baking soda together. Beat the shortening, brown sugar, sugar and vanilla in a mixer bowl until creamy. Add the eggs, beating until light and fluffy. Add the dry ingredients and oats gradually, beating until mixed. Stir in the chocolate chips. Drop by rounded teaspoonfuls onto a greased cookie sheet. Bake at 350 degrees for 8 to 10 minutes or until golden brown. Cool on the cookie sheet for 2 minutes. Remove to a wire rack to cool completely.

Makes 24 cookies

■

We all have an obligation to give something of ourselves to our community.

Cape Cod Oatmeal Cookies

■ ■ ■ ■ ■

1¹/₂ cups flour
¹/₂ teaspoon baking soda
1 teaspoon cinnamon
¹/₂ teaspoon salt
1 cup sugar
¹/₂ cup melted butter
¹/₂ cup melted lard
¹/₄ cup milk
1 egg, beaten
1 tablespoon molasses
1³/₄ cups rolled oats
1 cup raisins

*S*ift the flour, baking soda, cinnamon and salt into a bowl and mix well. Stir in the sugar, butter, lard, milk, egg and molasses. Add the oats and raisins and mix well. Drop by rounded tablespoonfuls onto a greased or nonstick cookie sheet. Bake at 350 degrees for 12 minutes or until the edges are brown. Add 1 to 2 additional cups oats and ¹/₄ cup flour for denser cookies.

Makes 24 cookies

Jeff Schultz

Susan Butcher

The owner of 150 dogs on her homestead in Eureka, Alaska, Susan Butcher is the first person to win the Iditarod dog sled race three consecutive times. She holds nine world records in various dog sled competitions, and in the 1990 racing season, Butcher raced more miles in one year than any other musher in history, totaling 2,250 miles. She has received numerous awards, including the Healthy American Fitness Award in 1988 from the U.S. Jaycees and the President's Counsel on Physical Fitness, and was named Professional Sportswoman of the Year by the Women's Sports Foundation for 1987 and 1988.

■

Energy and happiness will be yours, if you follow your dreams.

Cheryl Tiegs

Now a successful mother and designer, Cheryl Tiegs originally gained popularity as a model. Appearing on three Time *magazine covers as well as hundreds of other magazine covers in the United States and in Europe, she has had one of the most prolific modeling careers of all time. While still an active model, Cheryl Tiegs made the successful transition to designer. Her name has graced her successful line of clothing, eyeglass frames, fine jewelry, fashion watches, hosiery, socks, and shoes. The author of* Way to Natural Beauty, *she was the fashion, beauty, and fitness correspondent for "Good Morning America." Cheryl Tiegs has become a role model in the fitness arena as well, appearing in a* Sports Illustrated *exercise video.*

Reach for the stars. Make goals out of your dreams and work hard to make them a reality.

Classic Oatmeal Cookies with Ginger

2 tablespoons sugar
$^1/_4$ teaspoon cinnamon
$^3/_4$ cup flour
1 teaspoon freshly grated gingerroot, or
$^1/_4$ teaspoon ground ginger
$^1/_2$ teaspoon baking soda
$^1/_4$ teaspoon salt
$^1/_4$ teaspoon cinnamon
$^1/_4$ teaspoon nutmeg
$^3/_4$ cup butter or margarine
$^1/_2$ cup sugar
$^1/_2$ cup packed light brown sugar
1 egg
$^1/_2$ teaspoon vanilla extract
$1^1/_2$ cups quick-cooking oats
$^1/_2$ cup golden raisins, chopped
$^1/_2$ cup pecans, chopped

*C*ombine 2 tablespoons sugar and $^1/_4$ teaspoon cinnamon in a small bowl and mix well. Mix the flour, gingerroot, baking soda, salt, $^1/_4$ teaspoon cinnamon and nutmeg together. Beat the butter, $^1/_2$ cup sugar and brown sugar in a mixer bowl until fluffy. Add the egg, beating until blended. Beat in the vanilla. Stir in the flour mixture gradually. Fold in the oats, raisins and pecans. Drop by rounded teaspoonfuls onto a cookie sheet. Flatten each cookie with the bottom of a glass that has been buttered and dipped into the sugar and cinnamon mixture. Bake at 350 degrees for 8 to 10 minutes or until medium brown. Remove to a wire rack to cool.

Makes 24 cookies

Bonnie Blair's Peanut Butter Cookies

■ ■ ■ ■ ■

1 cup butter, softened
1 cup peanut butter
1/2 teaspoon salt
1 cup sugar
1 cup packed brown sugar
2 eggs, beaten
1 tablespoon milk
2 cups sifted flour
1/2 teaspoon baking soda

Combine the butter, peanut butter and salt in a mixer bowl and mix well. Add the sugar and brown sugar gradually, beating until creamy after each addition. Add the eggs and milk and mix well. Stir in a sifted mixture of the flour and baking soda. Drop by teaspoonfuls onto a greased cookie sheet; flatten with a fork. Bake at 325 degrees for 15 to 20 minutes or until brown. Remove to a wire rack to cool.

Makes 24 cookies

Bonnie Blair

One of America's most beloved athletes, Bonnie Blair is celebrated as the speedskater who has produced her best performances under pressure. She was the first American woman to win consecutive Winter Olympic gold medals. In 1994, Blair skated in her final Winter Olympics in Lillehammer, Norway, and swept the sprint races, winning the gold medal in both events. By capturing her sixth career Olympic medal, Bonnie emerged as U.S. history's most decorated Winter athlete, as well as the world record holder for the most gold medals (five) won by an American woman in any sport.

■

Everyone can better herself by finding something she loves to do and dedicating herself to it. Be willing to risk your pride and remember to keep a balance in your life, with the help of faith, friends and family.

George Lange Photography

Maida Heatter

The author of seven dessert books, Maida Heatter has received the James Beard Book Award twice— for Maida Heatter's Book of Great Cookies *and the* New York Times *bestseller,* Maida Heatter's Book of Great Chocolate Desserts. *Although her first love has always been cooking, she also studied fashion illustration at the Pratt Institute and has done fashion illustrating and indesigning, made jewelry, and painted. Teaching cooking classes in her home, department stores, and in cooking schools across the country, Maida Heatter prepared the desserts for the 1983 Summit of Industrialized Nations at Colonial Williamsburg, Virginia, for President Reagan and six other heads of state.*

▮

Bake Cookies—Happiness Is Baking Cookies!

Peanut Raisin Spice Cookies

▪ ▪ ▪ ▪ ▪

3 cups sifted unbleached flour
1 teaspoon baking powder
1 teaspoon baking soda
1 teaspoon ginger $^1/_2$ teaspoon salt
$^1/_2$ teaspoon cinnamon $^1/_2$ teaspoon nutmeg
1 cup unsalted butter $1^3/_4$ cups sugar
1 teaspoon vanilla extract   2 eggs
2 cups salted peanuts $2^1/_2$ cups raisins

*A*djust 2 oven racks to divide the oven into thirds. Line cookie sheets with baking parchment or foil shiny side up. Sift the flour, baking powder, baking soda, ginger, salt, cinnamon and nutmeg together. Beat the butter in a mixer bowl until creamy. Beat in the sugar and vanilla. Add the eggs and mix well. Add $^1/_2$ of the dry ingredients. Beat at low speed until blended. Stir in the remaining dry ingredients; dough will be stiff. Stir in the peanuts and raisins. Shape the dough using a 2-inch ice cream scoop, $^1/_4$-cup measuring cup or a large spoon. Arrange each mound $2^1/_2$ inches apart on the prepared cookie sheets; 6 cookies will fit on a 14x17-inch cookie sheet. Flatten the mounds formed with the ice cream scoop or $^1/_4$-cup measuring cup with a wet fork to $^1/_2$ inch thick. Roll the mounds formed with a large spoon into balls; flatten each ball into a $^1/_2$x$2^1/_2$-inch circle. Bake 2 cookie sheets at a time. Bake at 350 degrees for 18 minutes or until golden brown, rotating the cookie sheets once or twice top to bottom and front to back. Remove the cookies to a wire rack to cool. Store in an airtight container.

Makes 24 cookies

Reprinted with permission of Maida Heatter

Pecan Roll Cookies

■ ■ ■ ■ ■

1 cup margarine
$^1/_4$ cup confectioners' sugar
2 cups flour
1 tablespoon cold water
1 teaspoon vanilla extract
2 cups broken pecans
Confectioners' sugar to taste

*B*eat the margarine and confectioners' sugar in a mixer bowl until creamy. Add the flour, cold water and vanilla and mix well. Stir in the pecans. Shape with floured hands into date-like shapes. Arrange on a greased cookie sheet; crease lengthwise with a knife. Bake at 275 degrees for 1 hour. Roll the warm cookies in confectioners' sugar.

Makes 50 cookies

Elizabeth Dole

As president of the American Red Cross, Elizabeth Dole has dedicated her life to public service. Using advances in technology, she is in the midst of transforming the blood delivery system for the Red Cross, making it as safe and efficient as possible. She has served in the administrations of six presidents, holding two cabinet posts.

■

Some excellent advice for a fulfilling life was given to me by my grandmother, Mom Cathey, who taught that it was very important to always look for ways in your private life and your professional life to make a positive difference in the lives of others. Volunteer activities not only offer the opportunity to make that positive difference for others, but volunteers often find new meaning in their own lives. It's my hope that today's Girl Scouts will find a way to become future American Red Cross volunteers.

Elizabeth B. Terry

Chef and owner of Elizabeth on 37th Restaurant and Dessert Cafe in Savannah, Georgia, since 1981, Elizabeth Terry has a reputation as an innovator in the cuisine of the "new South" that is well established. Her devotion to classic southern cooking is such that she has extensively researched Savannah cooking of the 18th and 19th centuries. Profiled in numerous publications, Elizabeth Terry was also honored by the James Beard Foundation as the 1995 Perrier Jouët America's Best Chef: Southeast. Her other awards include the 1995 Ivy Award, given by Restaurants & Institutions, the DiRoNa Award, and Food and Wine *magazine's Top 25 Restaurants in America. Elizabeth on 37th, which she co-owns with her husband Michael, was named Savannah's Small Business of the Year in 1993.*

Chocolate Pecan Cookies

■ ■ ■ ■ ■

8 ounces sweet chocolate
1 tablespoon unsalted butter
2 eggs
³/₄ cup sugar
¹/₄ cup cake flour
¹/₄ teaspoon baking powder
¹/₄ teaspoon cinnamon
¹/₈ teaspoon salt
³/₄ cup pecan pieces
¹/₂ teaspoon vanilla extract

*C*ombine the chocolate and butter in a heatproof bowl. Place in a skillet of hot but not boiling water, stirring until melted. Be careful not to splash any water into the chocolate mixture or the chocolate will "seize" and will not melt properly. Beat the eggs in a mixer bowl until fluffy. Add the sugar 2 tablespoons at a time, beating constantly at low speed for 4 minutes. Sift the cake flour, baking powder, cinnamon and salt into a bowl and mix well. Fold into the egg mixture. Fold in the chocolate mixture. Stir in the pecans and vanilla. Drop by teaspoonfuls 2 inches apart onto a buttered cookie sheet. Place on the middle oven rack. Bake at 375 degrees for 3 minutes or until the cookies are shiny and puffed. Remove to a wire rack to cool. Store in an airtight container until ready to serve. The cookies will rise but still be soft in the center. When removed from the oven, they will fall, crack and remain chewy. Do not bake longer than 3 minutes. These are tiny rich chocolate delights that I feel should not be larger than a silver dollar.

Makes 24 cookies

Savannah Seasons: Foods and Stories from Elizabeth on 37th by
Elizabeth Terry and Alexis Terry. Doubleday, June, 1996.

Mexican Wedding Cookies
(Viscochos)

■ ■ ■ ■ ■

These cookies are generally served at weddings, but have transcended to all family gatherings.

2 cups shortening
5 egg yolks
1¹/₂ cups sugar
1 tablespoon freshly ground cinnamon
1¹/₂ teaspoons salt
6 cups flour
1 cup brandy, white wine or pineapple juice

Beat the shortening in a mixer bowl until light and fluffy. Beat in the egg yolks 1 at a time. Combine the sugar, cinnamon and salt in a small bowl. Reserve ¹/₂ cup of the mixture. Add the remaining cinnamon mixture to the egg yolk mixture, stirring well. Add the flour and brandy alternately, beginning and ending with the flour and beating well after each addition. Separate the dough into 4 portions. Chill, covered with plastic wrap, for 30 minutes. Roll out on a floured surface to ¹/₈-inch thickness; cut with a cookie cutter. Place on a cookie sheet. Bake at 400 degrees for 10 minutes or until light golden brown. Dust with the reserved cinnamon mixture. Place on a wire rack to cool.

Makes 60 cookies

Belen B. Robles

The history-making first woman president of the nation's oldest and largest Hispanic civil rights organization, Belen B. Robles has been an active member of the League of United Latin American Citizens (LULAC) for over 40 years. She has held several elected and appointed positions on both the local level and national level, and has been recognized as an outstanding leader in helping Hispanic Americans obtain civil and social justice for themselves and their families. Throughout her four decades of community involvement, Belen Robles has played an active role in insuring that the culture, history, and economic conditions of her constituents are not overlooked in the corridors of power.

■

Follow your dreams.
Nothing is impossible.

Constance Brown

Cynthia J. Salvato

A chef-instructor at Johnson and Wales University's prestigious International Pastry and Baking Institute, Cynthia Salvato has made desserts her calling card. She has left her mark, and pastries, at some of New England's finest restaurants, including Michela's in Cambridge, L'Espalier in Boston, and Le Grenier, a classical French restaurant on Martha's Vineyard where she spent a summer as the pastry chef. Chef Salvato was a member of the Distinguished Visiting Faculty committee of the culinary arts program at Boston University. She has published several articles and recipes, and is currently working on her first book, The Dowry Cookbook, *named after the Dowry Cookie Company, which she owns.*

■

Be honest. Own up to your mistakes (we all make them and learn from them). Work hard. Remember family is priority (number one). Try to give to those who are less fortunate.

Walnut Orange Biscotti

■ ■ ■ ■ ■

1 cup sugar
$1/2$ cup unsalted butter
1 egg, slightly beaten
1 tablespoon grated orange peel
$1^1/2$ teaspoons vanilla extract
$1/2$ teaspoon almond extract
$1^3/4$ cups flour
1 teaspoon baking powder
$1/8$ teaspoon salt
$1^1/2$ cups walnut pieces

*C*ream the sugar and butter in a mixer bowl until light and fluffy. Add the egg, beating well. Stir in the orange peel, vanilla and almond flavoring. Sift the flour, baking powder and salt together. Stir into the creamed mixture. Fold in the walnuts. Chill the dough for 2 hours to overnight. Shape into two $1^1/2$-inch-diameter logs on a floured surface. Place on a greased and floured cookie sheet. Bake at 350 degrees for 20 to 25 minutes or until golden brown. Remove from the oven and cool for 10 minutes. Remove from the cookie sheet and slice the logs with a serrated knife into $1/2$-inch slices. Place cut side down on the cookie sheet. Bake for 10 minutes longer. Cool on a wire rack; store in an airtight container.

Makes 24 cookies

Louvenia's Angel Food Cake

■ ■ ■ ■ ■

2 cups sugar
1 cup cake flour
15 egg whites, at room temperature
2 teaspoons vanilla extract
1¹/₂ teaspoons cream of tartar

*S*ift 1 cup of the sugar with the flour into a bowl; set aside. Beat the egg whites in a large mixer bowl until soft peaks form. Add the vanilla and cream of tartar. Add the remaining 1 cup of sugar 1 tablespoon at a time, beating until stiff peaks form. Fold in the flour mixture. Spoon into a 10-inch angel food cake pan. Bake at 350 degrees for 40 minutes. Invert onto a wire rack to cool completely before removing from the pan.

Serves 10

Nikki Giovanni

A poet who has authored 17 books and recorded six albums, Nikki Giovanni is a writer whose works were responsible for launching an army of Black pride in the early Seventies. She was described as a true revolutionary by one of her fans. Giovanni's most significant contribution to literature has been as a role model for young Black writers—females in particular. "She gave a voice to our experiences, and in so doing became a catalytic agent for a whole generation of writers to also speak up and out," wrote one fan.

■

Read! Read! Read! Let your heart and your dreams take you on an adventure. Always remember that, with hard work and determination, dreams do come true.

Anne Willan

Chef Willan founded La Varenne in Paris in 1975. Since 1991, she has operated at Chateau du Fey in Burgundy from June to October and at the Greenbrier in West Virginia from February through May. She has published her own successful cookbooks and been included in numerous others. She is an established lecturer, a respected food columnist and has appeared on nationally syndicated television and radio programs.

Don't hesitate to accept a challenge and enjoy an adventure.

Breton Butter Cake

Just think of Breton Butter Cake as the very best buttery shortbread you've ever tasted. You don't need a bowl to mix it, as it is worked like French pastry on a flat surface to form a soft dough, which bakes like a chewy biscuit. It keeps well for 2 to 3 days in an airtight container. You can eat it alone, or with berries or fruit. Remember, unsalted butter makes all the difference to this recipe: do not use salted varieties.

2 cups flour
1 cup unsalted butter, softened
2 cups sugar
6 egg yolks

*P*reheat the oven to 350 degrees. Brush a 9-inch tart pan with a removable bottom with a small amount of butter. Pour the flour onto the work surface, making a well in the center. Add the butter, sugar and 5$\frac{1}{2}$ of the egg yolks. Work the mixture for 1 to 2 minutes or until smooth. Continue to work the mixture for 2 to 3 minutes longer or until smooth and sticky. Place in the prepared pan, pressing the dough until smooth and flattened. Brush with the remaining egg yolk; trace a lattice pattern on the surface with a fork. Bake for 35 to 45 minutes or until golden brown and the edge pulls away from the side of the pan. Cool slightly and unmold onto a serving plate.

Serves 8

In and Out of the Kitchen in 15 Minutes or Less, Rizzoli 1995.

Spicy Carrot Cake

■ ■ ■ ■ ■

Allow the cake to stand for 1 day or even a day and half before slicing and serving as this substantially improves the flavor.

2 cups grated carrots
$^1/_2$ cup butter
1 cup sugar
$^1/_4$ cup water
1$^1/_4$ cups flour
$^1/_2$ tablespoon cinnamon
1 teaspoon ground cloves
$^3/_8$ teaspoon freshly ground nutmeg
$^1/_4$ teaspoon double-action baking powder
1 teaspoon baking soda
$^3/_8$ teaspoon ground allspice
$^1/_4$ teaspoon salt
1 egg

*C*ombine the carrots, butter, sugar and water in a heavy saucepan. Bring to a boil. Cook over medium heat for 5 minutes, stirring occasionally. Remove from heat and set aside to cool. Sift the flour, cinnamon, cloves, nutmeg, baking powder, baking soda, allspice and salt into a bowl. Beat the egg in a small mixer bowl until pale yellow. Combine the egg, sifted dry ingredients and the carrot mixture in a bowl, stirring just until mixed. Spoon into a greased 4x8-inch loaf pan. Bake at 350 degrees for 1 hour. Cool on a wire rack. Garnish with confectioners' sugar and slice into $^1/_2$-inch thick slices to serve.

Serves 12

Justice Ruth Bader Ginsburg

Nominated by President Clinton as Associate Justice of the United States Supreme Court, Ruth Bader Ginsburg took the oath of office on August 10, 1993. Prior to her appointment to the Supreme Court, she served from 1980 to 1993 on the bench of the United States Court of Appeals for the District of Columbia Circuit. In 1971, then-Professor Ginsburg was instrumental in launching the Women's Rights Project of the American Civil Liberties Union. Throughout the 1970s, she litigated a series of cases solidifying a constitutional principle against gender-based discrimination.

■

Aspire, and work hard to achieve your aspirations. Appreciate that, in our open society, no doors are closed to people willing to spend the hours of effort needed to make dreams come true.

Margaret Fox

Successful restaurateur, chef, and cookbook author, Margaret Fox has come a long way since her first culinary triumphs with French toast and rice pudding at the age of nine. Her magic with breakfast foods and her scrumptious desserts have won her accolades from writers and food critics across the country. Her book, Cafe Beaujolais, *chronicles the joys and pitfalls of owning a country restaurant.*

■

Probably one of the hardest and most important things in life is to be honest with yourself—about what your real feelings are, what you truly want to do and why. Don't be afraid to say "I don't know" or to make mistakes—this is how people learn. Laugh at your foibles. Know that every situation, no matter how terrible-seeming, contains an opportunity for growth.

Amazon Chocolate Cake

■ ■ ■ ■ ■

2 cups cold water
$^1/_2$ cup plus 2 tablespoons corn oil
1 tablespoon vanilla extract
2 tablespoons white vinegar or strained lemon juice
3 cups flour
$^2/_3$ cup unsweetened baking cocoa
2 teaspoons baking soda
2 cups sugar
1 teaspoon salt
2 ounces unsweetened chocolate
$1^1/_2$ tablespoons instant coffee
2 tablespoons water
1 cup unsalted butter, softened
2 cups sifted confectioners' sugar
1 egg yolk

*C*ombine 2 cups water, oil, vanilla and vinegar in a bowl. Whisk in a sifted mixture of the flour, cocoa, baking soda, sugar and salt. Pour the mixture through a strainer into a bowl, mixing well. Pour into 2 greased and lined 9-inch cake pans. Tap the pans gently to remove air bubbles. Bake at 350 degrees for 25 to 30 minutes or until the layers test done. Mix the chocolate, coffee powder and 2 tablespoons water in a double boiler. Cook over hot water until the chocolate melts; cool slightly. Pour into a food processor container fitted with an S-blade. Add the butter, confectioners' sugar and egg yolk. Process until smooth. Chill for 15 to 20 minutes or until of spreading consistency. Spread between the layers and over the top and side of the cooled cake.

Serves 12

White Chocolate Strawberry Roulade

■ ■ ■ ■ ■

6 eggs   1 egg yolk
$^1/_2$ cup sugar   Vanilla extract to taste
$^1/_2$ cup flour $^1/_2$ cup confectioners' sugar
6 ounces white chocolate   2 cups ricotta cheese
$^1/_2$ cup whipping cream   Zest of 1 orange
2 cups coarsely chopped fresh strawberries
12 ounces bittersweet chocolate
$1^1/_4$ cups whipping cream
4 ounces white chocolate, melted
$1^1/_4$ cups whipping cream, whipped

Caprial Pence

*Co-owner of Caprial's Bistro & Wine
since 1992, Caprial Pence has a
series on the Learning Channel
called "Caprial's Cafe" and a series
on Public Television called "Cooking
with Caprial." Her Bistro is a 28-seat
restaurant and retail wine store
serving both lunch and dinner.
Previously, she was Chef at Fullers
Restaurant at the Seattle Sheraton
Hotel and Towers, where she and two
staff members were the first Americans
to be invited to do a cooking exchange
in the former Soviet Union. The
recipient of several awards for her
cooking, she was named Best Chef in
the Northwest in 1990 by the James
Beard Foundation.*

■

*I would tell both young girls and young
women to believe in their worth and their
abilities. There will be people that will
both support and not support them in
their lives, but first of all they have to
support and believe in themselves. There
is no one that can take that away.*

Separate 3 eggs, reserving the egg whites in a mixer bowl. Beat the remaining eggs and yolks in a mixer bowl. Add the sugar and vanilla. Beat at high speed for 5 minutes or until light and pale yellow. Fold in the flour. Beat the reserved egg whites until soft peaks form. Fold into the egg yolk mixture. Pour into a greased 10x15-inch cake pan lined with parchment. Bake at 350 degrees for 20 to 30 minutes or until the cake tests done. Cool in the pan for several minutes. Dust a kitchen towel with the confectioner's sugar. Invert the cake onto the towel. Roll as for a jelly roll. Let stand until cool. Heat 6 ounces white chocolate in a double boiler over hot water until melted. Fold in the ricotta cheese, $^1/_2$ cup cream, orange zest and strawberries. Unroll the cake; spread with the filling and reroll. Chill in the refrigerator. Process the bittersweet chocolate in a food processor until chopped. Heat $1^1/_4$ cups cream to the boiling point in a saucepan. Pour through the feed tube, processing until smooth. Cool. Pour over the roulade. Chill until the chocolate is set. Drizzle with the remaining white chocolate. Chill until serving time. Place a dollop of the whipped cream on the side of each serving.

Serves 12

111

Lissa Doumani

Lissa Doumani always knew she wanted to own a restaurant. Born to a family of great cooks and wine-makers, she gained her experience in the kitchens of La Cienega Restaurant and Spago, both in Los Angeles. Currently, she co-owns the restaurant, Terra, with her fiancé and partner Hiro Sone. Besides consulting on the restaurant's dessert offerings, she is Terra's business manager and hostess.

Most successful women don't believe that they are successful, so they don't ever slow down, always trying to go further. The best rule I have learned is not to assume things are being done the way you like them to be. There is no better judge of what you want than you, so if you delegate responsibility still always keep an eye on how everything is going. But don't be afraid to enjoy your success— Remember to take time for yourself.

Chocolate Truffle Cake

■ ■ ■ ■ ■

Use six 4-inch rings, 8-ounce soufflé dishes or tuna cans with the tops and bottoms removed.

20 ounces bittersweet chocolate   **1 egg yolk**
3 ounces cream   **$\frac{1}{3}$ cup cognac**
9 ounces butter   **5 eggs, beaten**
1 cup plus 1 tablespoon sugar   **$\frac{1}{2}$ cup cornstarch, sifted**
1 tablespoon (about) cocoa powder

For the truffles: Melt 11 ounces of the chocolate in a double boiler over hot water. Cool slightly. Whisk in egg yolk just until blended. Bring the cream and cognac to a boil in a saucepan, stirring frequently. Whisk into the chocolate mixture. Pour into a deep bowl. Chill, covered, for 4 hours or until set. Scoop out with a $\frac{1}{2}$-inch melon ball cutter. Flatten into disks. Chill, covered, for up to 2 weeks.

For the cake: Melt 9 ounces of the chocolate and butter in a double boiler, stirring frequently. Whisk the eggs and sugar in a bowl until the sugar dissolves. Add the chocolate mixture, whisking until smooth. Fold in the cornstarch. Line a 10x15-inch sheet cake pan with parchment paper. Place rings on the paper. Spoon $\frac{2}{3}$ of the batter into the rings. Place 1 chocolate disk into each ring and cover with the remaining batter. Bake at 325 degrees for 14 to 16 minutes or until the top is crusty but the cake is still soft. Cool slightly. Remove the rings. Dust half of each serving plate with cocoa powder. Place cakes on plates. Serve with coffee or espresso ice cream. May reheat cakes at 350 degrees for 3 minutes. Shape any extra disks into balls and dust with cocoa powder.

Serves 6

Peppermint Patti

■ ■ ■ ■ ■

1¹/₂ pounds peppermints or starlite mints
3 cups whipping cream   4 cups milk   ¹/₂ cup sugar
2 tablespoons vanilla extract   6 egg yolks
1 cup sifted flour   2 cups sugar   ¹/₈ teaspoon salt
1 cup butter   3 ounces unsweetened chocolate
1 teaspoon vanilla extract
3 eggs, beaten   3 tablespoons sour cream
2 cups semisweet chocolate chips
1 cup whipping cream
8 ounces semisweet or dark bittersweet
chocolate, finely chopped

*C*ombine the peppermints, 3 cups cream and milk in the top of a double boiler. Cook over hot water until blended and the temperature reaches 200 degrees on a candy thermometer. Beat ¹/₂ cup sugar, 2 tablespoons vanilla and egg yolks in a bowl. Pour into the top of a double boiler. Heat gently over hot water just until warmed, stirring constantly. Add the peppermint mixture, whisking to combine. Chill for 8 to 10 hours. Pour into an ice cream freezer container. Freeze using manufacturer's directions. Butter a 10-inch cake pan; line with parchment paper. Mix the flour, 2 cups sugar and salt in a bowl. Melt the butter and unsweetened chocolate in a double boiler over hot water. Stir into the dry ingredients. Stir in 1 teaspoon vanilla, eggs, sour cream and chocolate chips. Pour into prepared pan. Bake at 350 degrees for 30 minutes. Cool in the pan for 45 minutes. Heat 1 cup whipping cream in a saucepan to just below the boiling point; remove from the heat. Add the semisweet chocolate, stirring until melted. Spoon 2 tablespoons of the chocolate sauce onto dessert plates. Place a slice of the cake on the sauce and top with a scoop of the ice cream.

Serves 12

Mary B. Sonnier

Born in New Orleans in 1958, Mary Blanchard Sonnier served as apprentice chef under Chef Paul Prudhomme, the master of South Louisiana cuisine. She runs her own restaurant, Gabrielle's (named after her daughter and her husband's grandmother) with her husband and partner Greg Sonnier, who is also an accomplished chef. Gabrielle's is a favorite among locals and visitors alike, noted for its excellence in contemporary cooking. Among many recognitions, Mary has also been honored by the Mayor as an outstanding citizen of New Orleans and she and husband Greg were named as two of "50 People to Watch" by New Orleans Magazine.

■

To set goals for yourself that are reasonable and then to achieve them, work hard; be good to yourself and others; use your imagination to gain success! Being a creative person has gotten me everywhere.

Al Weems Photography

Meridith Ford

A pastry chef, food writer, and teacher, Meridith Ford is currently writing a children's cookbook. Working professionally in the theatre, she began her training as a chef in 1986. Meridith was a pastry assistant at the Atlanta Hilton & Towers until she left to earn an occupational science degree in baking and pastry arts, and a degree in food marketing. Her food articles have been published in Chef *magazine,* Pastry Art & Design, *and* Fine Cooking. *Meridith is a member of the International Association of Culinary Professionals and the American Institute of Wine and Food.*

Strawberry-Filled Butter Cake

■ ■ ■ ■ ■

1¹/₂ ounces unflavored gelatin
1¹/₂ cups fresh lemon juice   2 teaspoons lemon zest
3 (14-ounce) cans sweetened condensed milk
1 quart heavy cream, whipped to medium peaks
1¹/₂ pints fresh strawberries, sliced
1 (2-layer) package butter cake mix
12 ounces white chocolate, finely chopped
2 cups egg whites   4 cups sugar
5 cups cold unsalted butter, cut into pieces

*S*often the gelatin in ¹/₂ cup lemon juice in a saucepan. Heat over low heat until the gelatin dissolves. Mix with 1 cup lemon juice, zest and condensed milk in a large bowl; cool. Fold in whipped cream and strawberries. Chill. Grease and flour one 6-inch, one 8-inch and one 12-inch round cake pan. Prepare cake mix using package directions. Pour into prepared cake pans. Bake at 350 degrees: 6-inch cake for 20 minutes; 8-inch cake for 25 to 30 minutes; 12-inch cake for 40 to 45 minutes. Cool in pans for 5 minutes; invert onto wire racks. Split the layers. Melt chocolate in a double boiler. Combine egg whites and sugar. Heat the egg mixture over simmering water to 110 degrees and until the sugar is no longer grainy, whisking constantly. Remove from heat. Beat at high speed until stiff peaks form. Beat at medium speed until cool. Add butter gradually, beating until smooth. (Mixture may separate, but continue beating.) Stir 1 to 2 cups mixture into the melted chocolate. Add to the egg mixture, beating until smooth and creamy. Spread the strawberry filling between split layers; secure with wooden picks. Place each cake on cardboard circle of the appropriate size. Frost with white chocolate mixture; chill. Assemble the layers, using clear pillars or cake columns.

Serves 20

Pound Cake

■ ■ ■ ■ ■

8 egg whites, at room temperature
2²/₃ cups sugar
16 ounces butter, softened
8 egg yolks
3¹/₂ cups sifted flour
¹/₂ cup coffee cream
1 teaspoon vanilla extract

*B*eat the egg whites in a mixer bowl until soft peaks form. Add 6 tablespoons of the sugar gradually, beating until stiff peaks form; chill in the refrigerator. Beat the butter in a mixer bowl until light and fluffy, adding the remaining sugar gradually. Add the egg yolks 2 at a time, beating well after each addition. Add the flour and cream alternately, beating until the mixture is light. Add the vanilla. Beat for 10 minutes longer on low speed. Fold in the egg whites gently. Spoon into a greased bundt pan. Bake at 325 degrees for 1¹/₂ hours. Cool in the pan for 10 minutes. Invert onto a cake plate.

Serves 16

Portia N. Byrd

A master storyteller, Portia Byrd is also an experienced librarian with backgrounds in library program planning and community relations. She is a founding member of the Coalition of 100 Black Women, Southwest Connecticut, and is an active volunteer for several organizations, including the Girl Scouts. Portia Byrd has won several awards and recognitions, including the United Nations Distinguished Service Award. She is a teacher of the art of storytelling, a featured storyteller for Black History Month, and an organizer of special programs for Martin Luther King Day.

■

Don't let an opportunity pass you by when you can do something good for someone, be it a stranger at your door or someone you know. You will be rewarded for the good you do when you don't have to think about whether or not you should do it.

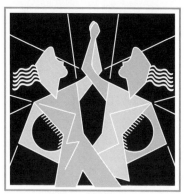

Mary Tillotson

Mary Tillotson is the host of "CNN & Co.," a half-hour talk show for policy experts hotly debating top news stories of the day. She covered the 1988 presidential election and worked both the Democratic and the Republican national conventions. Tillotson joined CNN in 1981 and served as White House correspondent during the Reagan Administration.

■

Know that life is a banquet and enjoy! And never ever let anyone, male or female, tell you gender is destiny: Marie Curie? Mary Cassatt? Sandra Day O'Conner? Eudora Welty? Barbara Tuchman? They excelled!

My Wene's Chocolate Pie

■ ■ ■ ■ ■

1$\frac{1}{4}$ cups sugar
$\frac{1}{2}$ cup flour
6 (heaping) tablespoons baking cocoa
$\frac{1}{8}$ teaspoon salt
2 cups water
3 egg yolks
$\frac{1}{4}$ cup butter, cut into pieces
1 baked (9-inch) pie shell
3 egg whites, at room temperature
6 tablespoons sugar

Combine 1$\frac{1}{4}$ cups sugar, flour, cocoa and salt in a heavy saucepan. Stir in 1 cup of the water or enough to make a paste. Add the egg yolks, beating well. Add the remaining water slowly, stirring constantly. Add the butter. Cook over low heat until the mixture is thick and begins to bubble, stirring constantly. Pour into the cooled pie shell; cool. Beat the egg whites in a mixer bowl until soft peaks form. Add 6 tablespoons sugar gradually, beating constantly until stiff peaks form. Spread over top of pie, sealing to edge. Bake at 350 degrees until the meringue is golden brown. May omit meringue and serve topped with sweetened whipped cream.

Serves 6

Penne's Pecan Pie

■ ■ ■ ■ ■

1 cup golden syrup
3 eggs, slightly beaten
1 cup packed brown sugar
(Mauritian Demarara, if possible)
2 teaspoons melted butter
1 teaspoon vanilla extract
¹/₈ teaspoon salt
1¹/₂ cups pecans
1 unbaked (9-inch) pie shell

Combine the syrup, eggs, brown sugar, butter, vanilla and salt in a large bowl; mix well. Fold in the pecans. Pour into the pie shell. Bake at 400 degrees for 15 minutes. Reduce the oven temperature to 350 degrees. Bake for 30 to 35 minutes longer or until the edge is set.

Serves 6

Honorable Penne Percy Korth

Nominated to the position of United States Ambassador Extraordinary and Plenipotentiary to Mauritius in 1989, Penne Korth was called later by the Prime Minister "the finest U.S. Ambassador we have had the pleasure and privilege of having in Mauritius." In 1988 she was chosen by President Bush as his first woman appointment to co-chair the American Bicentennial Presidential Inaugural. Subsequently, she has been the first woman elected as Honorary Rotarian in the Indian Ocean Region. She is a popular speaker and lecturer in the U.S. and abroad and is principal and co-founder of Firestone and Korth Ltd., an international consulting and events management firm in Washington, D.C.

■

A plaque on my desk reads: "It doesn't matter where a girl comes from, as long as she knows where she is going." Let your reach exceed your grasp—dreams really do come true!

Irene Young

Deidre McCalla

Releasing her third and most recent album in 1992, Everyday Heroes & Heroines, *Deidre McCalla has again proven herself to be a preeminent urban singer-songwriter and vivid essayist with a powerfully uncompromising vision. Of her first two releases,* "Don't Doubt It" *received two 1985 New York Music Award Nominations, and* "With a Little Luck" *was immediately pegged by the* Oakland Tribune *as one of the Ten Best Albums of the Year. Deidre McCalla is known to be a prolific performer, collaborator and creative artist who blends the richness of blues, jazz, folk and rock to bring a uniquely personal, even political tone to her music.*

■

Deep in the soul of every dreamer
Burns the silent flames of the Seeker.
No one can argue your visions. Or walk
through the worlds that you live in.
It's yours and yours alone
To seek each journey to end.
—Home in My Heart—

Deidre's Mom's Sweet Potato Pies

■ ■ ■ ■ ■

Sweet Potato Pie, like most of life, is more art than science. These measurements are only starting points; when I coerced the recipe out of mom, she simply said "Put in enough of everything until it tastes right." Your mileage may vary according to the sugar content of a particular bunch of potatoes, your own sweet tooth and what kind of mood you're in that day. It is essential to taste as you proceed and make adjustments accordingly. My mom also adds in cloves but I hate'em so I always leave them out. Mom also claims that yams are sweeter than sweet potatoes so I usually make yam pie, although I never call it that because it doesn't sound as cool. My mom's name is Julia.

4 to 5 pounds sweet potatoes (or yams)
$^1/_2$ cup butter   1 egg, beaten
1$^1/_2$ cups packed dark brown sugar
$^1/_4$ teaspoon vanilla extract   1 teaspoon nutmeg
$^1/_2$ teaspoon allspice   1 tablespoon (or more) milk
$^1/_8$ teaspoon salt
2 unbaked (9-inch) pie shells

Wash the sweet potatoes, cutting off and discarding the ends. Cut into quarters. Place in a large saucepan with water to cover. Bring to a boil. Cook until the potatoes are soft. Drain and cool slightly. Remove and discard the peels. Mash sweet potatoes with the butter in a large bowl. Add the egg, brown sugar, vanilla, nutmeg, allspice, milk and salt. Mash until smooth and creamy but slightly stiff. Spoon into the pie shells. Bake according to package directions for the pie shells. Cool.

Serves 12

Cindy Pawlcyn's S'more Pie

■ ■ ■ ■ ■

1 cup whole almonds, blanched
¹/₂ cup sugar   2 tablespoons butter
¹/₄ teaspoon salt   1 cup graham cracker crumbs
6 tablespoons melted butter   1 tablespoon sugar
6 ounces chocolate sauce   1 cup chopped chocolate
1 cup sugar   2 tablespoons corn syrup
²/₃ cup water   1¹/₂ envelopes unflavored gelatin
¹/₄ cup warm water   3 egg whites, at room temperature
¹/₂ teaspoon vanilla extract
4 graham crackers, broken into bite-sized pieces

*C*ombine the almonds, ¹/₂ cup sugar, 2 tablespoons butter and salt in a nonstick pan. Cook over medium-high heat until caramelized, stirring constantly. Pour the mixture onto a marble slab or a waxed-paper-lined baking sheet. Break into small pieces when cool. Press a mixture of the graham cracker crumbs and 6 tablespoons butter into a 9-inch pie plate. Sprinkle with 1 tablespoon sugar. Pour in ¹/₂ of the chocolate sauce. Top with ¹/₂ cup of the caramelized almond pieces and half the chopped chocolate. Bring 1 cup sugar, corn syrup and ²/₃ cup water to a boil in a saucepan. Cook to 240 degrees on a candy thermometer. Soften the gelatin in a small amount of cold water. Dissolve the softened gelatin in ¹/₄ cup warm water in a saucepan; keep warm. Beat the egg whites in a mixer bowl until soft peaks form. Add the syrup mixture gradually, beating constantly. Add the gelatin mixture and the vanilla, beating until cool. Spread a ¹/₂-inch layer of the marshmallow mixture over the chopped chocolate. Layer with the remaining chocolate sauce, graham cracker pieces, remaining chopped chocolate and remaining marshmallow mixture. Bake at 500 degrees until hot and light brown.

Serves 6

Mark Estes

Cindy Pawlcyn

Executive chef and owner of six California restaurants, Cindy Pawlcyn has been working in professional kitchens since she was 13. In 1988, she was inducted into "Who's Who of Cooking America." As a sous chef at prestigious restaurants around the country, she has been featured in Food and Wine's *"Top Twenty-Five Chefs,"* Bon Appetit's *"Cooking Class," and* Gourmet's *"Chefs Across America." Her book,* The Fog City Diner Cookbook, *1993, features recipes that have made this diner famous.*

■

I remember well my own days of being a Girl Scout. Some of my fondest memories are of having S'mores around a campfire. I am pleased to share my recipe for S'more Pie because the inspiration comes from those memories. I believe it is a good example of how something you enjoy as a child can lead you to a successful venture as an adult.

Felicia R. Pritchett

A baking and pastry chef who specializes in wedding cakes, Felicia Pritchett is on the cutting edge of wedding cake design. At Takes the Cake, Inc., the company she owns, Felicia is likely to create a wedding cake as unusual as a chocolate pecan sponge cake with a layer of raspberry purée, coated with white chocolate ganache and served with a caramel champagne sauce. She recently competed in the third annual Domaine Carneros Wedding Cake Competition in New York City, and has won first-place awards in food shows from Boston to Chicago. Felicia is a member of the International Cake Exploration Society and the Rhode Island Cake Decorators Club, and her recipes have graced the pages of newspaper food sections across the country.

Caramel Champagne Sauce

■ ■ ■ ■ ■

1$\frac{1}{2}$ cups sugar
1 to 2 tablespoons unsalted butter
$\frac{1}{4}$ to $\frac{1}{2}$ cup whipping cream
Champagne to taste

Melt the sugar $\frac{1}{2}$ cup at a time in a heavy saucepan over medium heat, stirring constantly with a wooden spoon. Remove from the heat when the melted sugar is very light brown in color. Slowly add the butter and cream alternately, stirring constantly. Heat gently if necessary to melt the ingredients together. Stir in as much Champagne as desired for taste and consistency. Serve warm.

Makes 8 (2-tablespoon) servings

Nutritional Profiles

■ ■ ■ ■ ■

Pg #	Recipe Title (Approx Per Serving)	Cal	Prot (g)	Carbo (g)	T Fat (g)	% Cal from Fat	Chol (mg)	Fiber (g)	Sod (mg)
10	Baked Brie	614	28	42	39	55	125	2	801
11	Sweet Potato Dip	76	3	18	0	0	0	1	35
12	Tomato Salsa	8	<1	2	<1	11	0	<1	56
13	Shari Lewis' Mozzarella Marinara*	287	18	19	15	49	104	<1	975
14	Snake Bites*	429	17	72	7	15	204	4	258
15	Mom's Basic BBQ Sauce	28	<1	3	2	53	0	<1	90
16	Beet Soup (Barszcz)	262	10	16	18	62	88	2	1053
17	Broccoli and Cauliflower Soup	154	8	15	7	42	0	3	875
18	Curried Ginger Carrot Soup	74	1	9	4	45	10	2	766
19	Johnny Bob's Chili	443	29	51	13	26	63	15	1552
20	Kay's Shadywood Showdown Chili	338	37	18	13	35	95	5	647
21	Pamela Peters' Chili	830	50	51	50	53	152	15	989
22	Spicy Crab Soup	324	29	34	6	17	60	3	3436
23	Cold Gazpacho	147	3	17	9	51	0	4	488
24	Creole Gumbo New Orleans Style	299	29	17	14	41	153	4	1349
25	Minestrone	248	9	29	12	42	1	7	1487
26	Basic Potato Soup	194	3	36	5	21	0	3	542
27	Winter Squash and Pear Soup	214	5	25	12	46	32	6	919
28	Watercress Soup	306	14	10	24	69	102	1	854
29	Port Clyde Broccoli Salad Sandwich	212	8	34	6	24	4	4	336
30	Three-Bean Salad	394	7	45	22	49	0	9	1196
31	Gran Salad	282	4	28	18	56	18	1	96
32	Curried Chicken Salad with Mangoes	603	60	41	24	35	150	6	278
33	Pang Pang Chicken Salad	192	22	3	10	48	62	1	299
34	Summer Tomato Salad	225	3	15	18	69	<1	3	112
36	Beef Tenderloin*	272	23	25	10	31	56	3	147
37	Nina's Beef Stew	469	46	30	16	30	136	5	1061
38	1-2-3 Stew	445	65	7	16	33	169	<1	899
39	Phyllis Diller's Tamale Pie	289	18	21	15	47	54	3	653
40	Meat Loaf	336	29	15	18	48	139	1	1079
41	Venison and Wild Rice Casserole	290	27	40	3	8	75	2	61
42	Jessye Norman's Corsican Chicken	709	56	34	38	47	151	5	448
43	Chicken Adobo	228	34	3	8	34	100	<1	782
44	Green Chicken Chilaquiles	624	41	31	38	54	92	3	3254

Pg #	Recipe Title (Approx Per Serving)	Cal	Prot (g)	Carbo (g)	T Fat (g)	% Cal from Fat	Chol (mg)	Fiber (g)	Sod (mg)
45	West African Groundnut Stew	469	34	37	22	41	75	6	689
46	Raspberry Chicken	229	27	23	3	13	73	3	263
47	Chicken with Cashew Nuts	506	32	19	34	59	72	2	740
48	Turkey Enchilada Casserole	269	16	21	13	44	49	2	849
49	Russian Turkey Meatball Stroganoff	369	41	66	17	26	240	2	1074
50	Stuffed Flounder Rolls	632	50	16	36	52	257	2	1263
51	Mint and Basil Marinated Salmon	643	32	31	45	62	161	5	171
52	Salmon Wrapped in Grape Leaves	642	41	21	45	62	119	2	97
53	Sesame Crusted Swordfish	970	54	50	62	57	91	5	350
54	Crab and Couscous Cakes	522	20	39	33	56	91	3	382
55	Shrimp and Tasso with Five-Pepper Jelly*	1081	21	31	100	81	375	3	1596
56	Lemon Pepper Barbecue Shrimp	310	5	18	28	73	35	1	44
57	Thai Curry Sea Scallops	577	37	35	34	51	62	4	955
58	Barbara's "Stay Fit" Angel Hair Pasta	566	32	100	4	6	118	7	554
59	Penne with Corn and Uncooked Tomato Sauce	697	18	107	23	30	0	8	38
60	Pasta with Beans and Pancetta	529	21	87	12	19	5	11	511
61	Tomato Basil Pasta	714	24	93	28	35	51	4	1178
62	Tortellini with Sun-Dried Tomato Pesto	998	29	64	72	64	88	3	1508
63	Hot Things*	427	19	27	28	57	73	3	935
64	Welsh Rarebit	790	38	39	54	61	167	2	1677
66	Cauliflower and Cheese Casserole	172	13	18	5	28	24	2	747
67	Eggplant Casserole	161	8	12	9	51	25	2	500
68	Grits and Greens	405	15	23	29	63	91	4	538
69	Cheese-Stuffed Potatoes	93	5	17	1	6	2	1	121
70	Oprah's Potatoes	254	6	53	2	7	3	4	177
71	Stewed Rice (Arroz Guisado Basico)	397	17	60	9	21	86	2	1098
72	Baked Risotto with Eggplant	369	13	34	20	48	36	5	860
73	Tomato, Basil and Cheese Tart	613	22	28	47	68	152	3	1204
74	Veggie and Rice Stir-Fry	194	5	35	4	18	0	3	528
75	Vegetable Terrine	316	11	21	21	60	216	2	513
76	Basic White Bread Recipe	130	4	26	1	8	1	1	183
77	Meringue Coffee Cake	298	7	55	6	19	145	0	84
78	Gnocchi Fritti*	761	25	150	6	7	6	8	384
79	Jalapeño Cheese Corn Bread	229	7	26	11	42	42	1	496
80	Nutty Nutmeg Muffins	180	5	21	9	43	49	1	187
81	Low-Fat Oat Bran Muffins	266	7	43	11	32	0	6	195
82	Washington Family Waffles	339	8	25	24	62	151	1	426
84	Bête Noire	641	8	56	44	58	164	3	65

Pg #	Recipe Title (Approx Per Serving)	Cal	Prot (g)	Carbo (g)	T Fat (g)	% Cal from Fat	Chol (mg)	Fiber (g)	Sod (mg)
85	Sour Cherry Blintzes	1092	22	102	65	53	440	3	631
86	Tartufo Ice Cream	352	7	34	26	59	103	5	41
87	Chocolate Bread Pudding	629	10	54	44	60	177	3	203
88	Crème Brûlée	465	6	39	33	62	250	0	175
89	Pavlova	227	2	31	11	43	41	2	31
90	Stuffed Chayote	266	7	40	11	34	112	3	34
91	Red White and Blue Cobbler	431	4	90	8	17	3	3	279
92	Peanut Butter Truffles	446	8	30	36	68	59	2	82
93	The Ultimate Brownie	260	2	21	20	67	54	1	11
94	Lemon Squares	61	1	8	3	42	19	<1	34
95	Alfajores de Maicena	244	4	41	7	26	56	<1	130
96	Alexis' Brown Sugar Chocolate Chip Cookies	191	2	26	10	45	38	1	112
97	Blue Ribbon Chocolate Chip Cookies	133	1	17	7	46	22	1	73
98	Hillary Clinton's Chocolate Chip Cookies	248	3	31	14	47	18	2	133
99	Cape Cod Oatmeal Cookies	183	2	24	9	43	24	1	106
100	Classic Oatmeal Cookies with Ginger	147	2	18	8	47	24	1	103
101	Bonnie Blair's Peanut Butter Cookies	233	4	25	14	51	39	1	199
102	Peanut Raisin Spice Cookies	298	6	40	14	41	38	2	153
103	Pecan Roll Cookies	85	1	5	7	71	0	<1	43
104	Chocolate Pecan Cookies	112	2	13	6	50	21	1	31
105	Mexican Wedding Cookies (Viscochos)	146	2	15	8	50	18	<1	54
106	Walnut Orange Biscotti	151	2	17	9	51	19	1	29
107	Louvenia's Angel Food Cake	220	6	47	1	5	<1	<1	118
108	Breton Butter Cake	555	6	74	27	43	221	1	10
109	Spicy Carrot Cake	204	2	31	8	36	38	1	210
110	Amazon Chocolate Cake	589	5	78	31	45	59	3	320
111	White Chocolate Strawberry Roulade	668	14	53	49	63	231	3	111
112	Chocolate Truffle Cake	1082	14	90	82	62	325	3	415
113	Peppermint Patti	1176	13	132	75	54	322	4	298
114	Strawberry-Filled Butter Cake	1198	13	109	82	60	252	1	315
115	Pound Cake	477	6	53	27	51	173	1	269
116	My Wene's Chocolate Pie	529	9	79	21	40	127	2	291
117	Penne's Pecan Pie	656	7	88	33	44	112	2	315
118	Deidre's Mom's Sweet Potato Pies	519	4	84	19	32	49	6	326
119	Cindy Pawlcyn's S'more Pie	731	11	101	35	41	46	3	433
120	Caramel Champagne Sauce	222	<1	38	8	33	28	0	6

*Nutritional information does not include oil for frying.

Index

■ ■ ■ ■ ■

Tell Us About Yourself

■ ■ ■ ■ ■

We invite you to share your Recipes For Success. Send us your words of wisdom or share your story about how you became a successful woman. This information will be shared with the Girl Scout organization in your community. Please return to the address below.

_____

_____

_____

_____

_____I have been involved in Girl Scouting in the following ways:

_____

_____

_____I am interested in mentoring/sharing my skills with girls in my community.

_____(_____)_____
Name   Phone

_____
Address   City   State   Zip

_____
Occupation   Company Name

If you would like additional copies of *Recipes For Success*, please contact:

Patriots' Trail Girl Scout Council
95 Berkeley Street
Boston, Massachusetts 02116
(617) 482-1078 or (800) 882-1662

Photocopies accepted.